THE BRIDGE

Moving from Increasing Chaos to Future Peace during the Next Economic Crisis

By: S. Renee Felder

Edited by: Kelly Beasley

DISCLAIMER

The Bridge/The Cover Club/Joseph Colony/Savutax Consulting, Inc. is not a registered investment adviser or registered broker-dealer nor does it endorse or recommend the services of any investment adviser or brokerage company or provide any investment advice or brokerage services. *The Bridge/The Cover Club/Joseph Colony/Savutax Consulting, Inc.* operates as a publisher/instructor and all information provided in this book, our articles, workshops, blog posts or websites are impersonal and for informational purposes only, and should not be construed as an offer or solicitation to buy or sell any security, metal, fiat currency or crypto currency. You should always pray for guidance, conduct your own research, and consult with licensed investment professionals, attorneys, and accountants before making any investment or major monetary decisions. While a security, metal, fiat currency or crypto currency's past performance may be analyzed in our writings, blog posts, websites or workshops, past performance should not be considered indicative of future results. To the maximum extent permitted by law, *The Bridge/The Cover Club/Joseph Colony/Savutax Consulting, Inc.* disclaims any and all liability in the event that any information, prophecy, commentary, analysis, opinions, advice, and/or recommendations in our books, articles, blogs, websites or workshops prove to be inaccurate, incomplete or unreliable, or result in, directly or indirectly, any investment or other losses. *The Bridge/The Cover Club/Joseph Colony/Savutax Consulting, Inc.* and/or its officers, directors, analysts, and other contractors or employees may or may not have positions in securities, investments and/or speculations referenced in this book, our articles, blog posts or websites.

This publication is designed to provide general information regarding the subject matter covered. However, laws and practices often vary from state to state and are subject to change. Because each factual situation is different, specific advice should be tailored to an individual's particular circumstances. For this reason, the reader is instructed to consult with his or her own advisor regarding their own specific situations.

The author has taken reasonable precautions in the preparation of this book and believes the facts presented herein are accurate as of the date it was written. However, neither the author nor the publisher assume any responsibility for any errors or omissions. The author and publisher specifically disclaim any liability resulting from the use or application of the information contained in this book, and the information is not intended to serve as legal advice related to individual situations.

> "I sometimes place a bridge between lack and abundance so that there is provision during the waiting period. But I do not abandon My people. Recognize My infinite ways as I am showing them. Learn to see Me in every situation. If you see Me and know My voice you will see the provision. I the LORD your God will provide for you."
>
> — Word from the Lord, October 2006

ACKNOWLEDGEMENTS

I would like to thank everyone who has been standing and praying with me through the process of writing this book. I would specifically like to thank Sharon Louise for her support, creativity, and input regarding the title and her contribution to help explain a derivative to the average person. I want to thank Gabriel Arosemena for designing the book interior, book cover and back. He is an anointed prophetic voice and was able to apply what he saw in the spirit to paper through his natural talent as a marketing designer. Lastly, I want to thank Kelly Beasley my editor and friend. Her contextual insights, fact checking, and editing skills helped me tremendously in completing this project.

TABLE OF CONTENTS

Disclaimer ii
Word from the Lord, October 2006 iii
Acknowledgements iv
Preface vi
Introduction x
Prophecy, October 23, 2006 xv
Vision, October 21, 2006 xx
Chapter One: Fear Not! 1
Chapter Two: America's Looming Financial Transition 7
Chapter Three: What will Happen with the Banks? 9
Chapter Four: What is a Derivative? 17
Chapter Five: Hyperinflation – What is It? 29
Chapter Six: Historical Case Studies – Economic Collapse 33
Chapter Seven: The Coming Paradigm Shift for America 51
Chapter Eight: The First Wave – Rents 61
Chapter Nine: The Second Wave – Hyperinflation 69
Chapter Ten: Preparation for Dark Days Ahead 77
Chapter Eleven: Wealth will Not Disappear; It will be Transferred 81
Chapter Twelve: *The Bridge* Currency Kit™ 83
Chapter Thirteen: How to Exchange Currency 91
Chapter Fourteen: Financial Triage 97
Chapter Fifteen: Conclusion 107
Appendix A: Representation of Supply and/or Stockpile List for Economic Collapse 111
About the Author 112

PREFACE

"A Bridge can still be built, while the bitter waters are flowing beneath."

Poet Anthony Liccione[1]

The Bridge is a prophetic word of what is to come regarding the U.S. economy as well as an instruction tool on how to strategize and prepare. Much of what is written herein – both historical and current events – are not new subjects for the reader. As such, they are summarized in hopes of persuading the reader that fulfillment of the prophetic words the Lord spoke to me is imminent.

One important note I want to emphasize is that the focus of this book is on the American and global economic climate. I make the assumption that governments and their leaders made decisions that influenced the outcome of their economic positions. I connect no political affiliation to this research, nor is it my intention to sway the reader politically regarding the topics within these pages.

One of the challenges in writing The Bridge is that many different perspectives about the history of economic and political events exist. Thus, The Bridge could have taken on many different tones or themes, any one of which would have sparked the reader with thought-provoking content. That being said, I made every effort to stay in my lane. Meaning, I tried to stay focused on the prophecies and topics God gave me. To that end, I did not include very many other prophetic voices, not because I don't think God has spoken to them, but because I do not want to engage in comparisons. I know there are many who have been shown similar

---

1 Editors, "Anthony Liccione Quotes," Success Story. https://successstory.com/quote/anthony-liccione (accessed February 22, 2019).

things. I do not suggest that I stand alone in receiving prophetic words. I am doing my best to obey HIS voice regarding how I am supposed to present the information contained in these pages.

I am not a professional historian or economist, or even a theologian, but I did my due diligence in research to support in the natural what I have been shown in the spirit. The book's purpose is not to give a historic or economic lesson. The information contained herein is intended to provide support for the prophetic words the Lord has given me. I mention just enough information and historical data to make my point.

There are many catalysts that will affect the impending economic collapse. But what is mentioned within these pages is what God specifically told me to focus on.

Bible passages used herein are quoted from either the King James Version ("KJV") or the New King James Version ("NKJV"). When I refer to the Lord, I am referring to Jesus the Messiah, the only begotten Son of the Most High God[2]. Here, in part, is what the Bible says about Him:

> *"And He is the head of the body, the church, who is the beginning, the firstborn from the dead, that in all things He may have the preeminence."*
>
> Colossians 1:18 (NKJV)

> *"But I would have you know, that the head of every man is Christ."*
>
> 1 Corinthians 11:3 (KJV)

---

2 John 3:16 (NKJV).

> *"For the husband is head of the wife, even as Christ is the head of the church; and He is the savior of the body."*
>
> Ephesians 5:23 (KJV)

"Christ," by definition is the anointed, the Messiah, the Son of God[3]. The "church" refers to the ekklēsia, or everyone who believes that Jesus is Messiah, the only begotten Son of God[4]. The "body" refers to people closely united into one family or society[5].

RECEIVING PROPHECIES

The prophecies God gave to me came in dreams, visions, and as rhēma words. The Holy Spirit delivered these rhēma words to me. Rhēma, by definition means "utterance or a saying of a message, a narrative concerning some occurrence."[6]

The Bridge is not a Bible study, nor is it my intent to enter into a debate about scripture or religious beliefs. My intention is to provide a brief background of some of the terminology and titles used, as well as a small glimpse into this writer's faith to allow the reader to follow along with minimal confusion.

YOU DECIDE

As you read, it does not matter to me whether you believe the content herein fully, partially, or at all. Within these pages, there are multiple secular references to information that supports the prophecies God gave to me. What I say now,

---

3   Strong's Concordance, G5547 – "Christos."
4   Strong's Concordance, G1577 – ekklēsia."
5   Strong's Concordance, G4983 – "sōma."
6   Strong's Concordance, G4487 – "rhēma."

and again later in the book regarding how things will play out in our economy, is partly what I have heard from the Lord, and partly the result of logical reasoning based on historical data, economic cycles, and my own opinion. However, it is my hope that readers will take very seriously the prophecies contained herein, and immediately begin taking action steps to secure a safety net for themselves and their loved ones.

GETTING PREPARED

I would like to make a general statement in regards to economic preparedness. There is no such thing as a one size fits all financial preparedness strategy, approach, or plan. The reader may decide to apply some of the strategies, all of the strategies, or a completely different strategy from those contained in this book. There is no right or wrong way to prepare. Readers are encouraged to pray and inquire of God for His strategies to be imparted to them, specific to their own circumstances.

INTRODUCTION

> *"Of all the wonderful but critical things for which these Josephs will have responsibility, we cannot overlook their importance to the Church. They will arise as men and women of incredible wisdom and vessels through which the seven Spirits of God will operate. Therefore, they will speak and act like living oracles from the Father above."*
>
> Nita (LaFond) Johnson[7]

Although this book can benefit anyone, it is specifically written for those who are called to or endowed with the Joseph anointing. These anointed ones are *the bridge*-builders called to shepherd people from the current economic structure to the next one in the wake of America's approaching economic collapse.

JOSEPH ANOINTING DEFINED

Jacob's youngest son, Joseph was a prophet gifted by God to interpret dreams. God anointed him with wisdom and understanding to make strategic decisions at a critical time in world history. The story of Joseph begins in Genesis 37. In summary, Egypt's Pharaoh received two dreams in the same night that greatly troubled him. Pharaoh inquired of his magicians and wise men. But they could not interpret his dreams. So they sent for Joseph who provided the interpretations to Pharaoh.

"And, behold, he stood by the river. Suddenly there

---

[7] Nita (LaFond) Johnson, Melchizedek, The New Millennium Priesthood, (California: Eagle's Nest Publishing, 2008), p. 264.

> *came up out of the river seven cows, fine looking and fat; and they fed in the meadow. Then behold, seven other cows came up after them out of the river, ugly and gaunt, and stood by the other cows on the bank of the river. And the ugly and gaunt cows ate up the seven fine looking and fat cows. So Pharaoh awoke. He slept and dreamed a second time; and suddenly seven heads of grain came up on one stalk, plump and good. Then behold, seven thin heads, blighted by the east wind, sprang up after them. And the seven thin heads devoured the seven plump and full heads. So Pharaoh awoke, and indeed, it was a dream."*
>
> Genesis 41:1-7 (NKJV)

Joseph informed Pharaoh that both dreams held the same meaning. He also said that since the dream came twice, the events that were about to take place had been established by God. In other words, they were certain to happen. Egypt and all the land would have seven years of great prosperity followed by seven years of famine so severe, that all previous prosperity would be forgotten.

But God didn't just give Joseph the interpretation of Pharaoh's dreams. He also provided the answer to the problem those dreams presented:

> *" 'Now therefore, let Pharaoh select a discerning and wise man, and set him over the land of Egypt. Let Pharaoh do this, and let him appoint officers over the land, to collect one-fifth of the produce of the land of Egypt in the seven plentiful years.*

> *And let them gather all the food of those good years that are coming, and store up grain under the authority of Pharaoh, and let them keep food in the cities. Then that food shall be as a reserve for the land for the seven years of famine which shall be in the land of Egypt; that the land may not perish during the famine.' So the advice was good in the eyes of Pharaoh and in the eyes of all his servants. And Pharaoh said to his servants, 'Can we find such a one as this, a man in whom is the Spirit of God?' Then Pharaoh said to Joseph, 'Inasmuch as God has shown you all this, there is no one as discerning and wise as you.' "*
>
> Genesis 41:33-39 (NKJV)

God gave Joseph a strategy for Egypt – store up enough food and provisions during the coming years of plenty in order to feed people during the impending famine. Through this strategy, God used Joseph to help all of Egypt as well as people from surrounding nations to survive during seven long years of relentless famine.

In recognition of Joseph's wise counsel, Pharaoh made Joseph second-in-command of his kingdom, to specifically oversee the implementation of God's strategies for surviving the coming famine. Under Joseph's leadership, during these years of plenty, Egypt got ready.

As this famine took hold in the earth, people from surrounding areas, including Joseph's family, the household of Jacob (Israel) came to Egypt to purchase food. As the famine wore on, people ran out of money to buy food, so they bartered their livestock, and later their land, in order to survive. This was the price that Egyptians and surrounding nations' peoples were willing to pay to keep from starving.[8] There are two points I want to emphasize about Joseph's story:

1) Joseph planned and oversaw the stockpiling and distribution of provisions/food for the all the people, including his own family. Without this provision, hundreds, if not thousands of people would have starved to death.

2) Wealth was transferred from other peoples and nations into Egypt's coffers during the years of famine. Those who were not prepared lost their wealth. Yet, Joseph and the household of Israel not only had provision of food, but were also given "the best of the land."[9]

Today in America, we are experiencing years of plenty. Soon however, years of financial famine will come. Although I don't know the specific timing, I believe America will begin experiencing pronounced economic shakings around 2022. Some parts of the country will fare better for a while longer than others. Even now, some Americans are experiencing financial adversity. But this reality is not apparent to everyone yet. In a few years' time, however, the entire country will see the evidence of this financial difficulty because most of us will be experiencing it as well – unless you are prepared.

Nathan Shaw describes the Joseph anointing this way:

"*The nations are entering a time of transition and change.*

---
8 Genesis 47:15-20 (KJV).
9 Genesis 47:6 (King James Version).

We should not be afraid. God has prepared many "Josephs" in advance. Joseph was God's secret weapon. He was used to save the ancient world during a time of extreme famine. Some of these Josephs are already being positioned to handle future crises. Other Josephs will come forth in the midst of crises. Joseph was both prophetic and entrepreneurial. This made him unique. Usually prophets are prophets and entrepreneurs are entrepreneurs. In Joseph, these two anointings are combined."[10]

If you have the Joseph anointing, you may be called to assist your family, friends, church, community, or an entire people group, city, or nation to survive during the approaching economic collapse. However, it is likely you are called specifically to a small group. You may be given a specific anointing to shepherd in the area of housing, food, finances, or something else pertaining to livelihood and survival.

The Bridge is a clarion call to the Josephs in the Body of Christ. When the next financial crisis hits, America will enter into some very dark days. Our Father in Heaven wants us to get ready **now** for the economic devastation we will need to weather. My hope is that as you read this book, you will pray, rise up to answer the clarion call, and start to prepare for what's coming.

---

10 Nathan Shaw, "The Joseph Anointing: Prophetic and Entrepreneurial," The Elijah List, January 2, 2017. http://www.elijahlist.com/words/display_word.html?ID=17236 (accessed February 1, 2019).

PROPHECY GIVEN ON OCTOBER 23, 2006

I, the LORD your God, am distressed by what I see. My people no longer know Me. They know not of My works, but count it their own. They worship Me and other idols, too. They treat Me as they do other gods and discard Me at will. I am distressed. Yet I cannot go back to the old ways as I have sent My Son to redeem them. But they do not believe. They do not accept My redemption. Yet My Son has redeemed them.

My own people are disobedient. The work of the Kingdom goes undone. I raise up one leader after another yet very few know My heart. They act in their own strength and not by the Holy Spirit which I sent. And yet I love them all; Like a mother who loves her disobedient child. Even I pray to Myself for My people. Rise up! I pray thee! Rise up for the time is at hand. The world is changing rapidly. My people must be ready. Superficial belief is no longer acceptable. Deep-rooted faith is a must. Warriors for the Kingdom are necessary.

Learn My voice and know My voice. Discard your worldly debt and possessions. Free yourself for My work. Be ready to move at a moments' notice. Diversify your currency. Diversify your wealth. Possessions must be left behind.

Free yourself from distractions and sit with Me. I will give you methods and strategies to move forward. I want My people prepared. They are distinguished because they hear My voice and obey. They will lead and others will follow. The time is at hand. Let being debt-free be a way of life.

First and foremost, My people must put Me before anything else.

Second, hear and obey My instructions. I will deliver them

through My chosen prophets and apostles. I will tell you in your quiet time. The venue of My instructions will confirm one another. Be wary of instruction that is unconfirmed for it is not from Me. I will not lead My people astray and I will not contradict Myself.

Third, become debt-free. Your methods will not be the same. One will work. Another will pray and be blessed. Don't trouble yourself about your neighbor. What I instruct you to do will work for you. What I instruct your neighbor to do will not work for you. You must seek Me. I have made you all unique. Not drones, but unique. Yet, each one of you is made in My image. Each of you has a part of Me woven into your character, your DNA.

I speak as in the old because you are like Old Testament babies. Have you forgotten that My son bore your sins on the cross? You are steeped in legalism as in the days of Moses. Do you not know that you are free? Through My son, you are free.

But My people have misunderstood freedom. My people have abused freedom. And yet My son has already died and risen for the sins of the earth. My Spirit is ever present but mostly ignored.

I am everywhere by My Spirit. Why do you ignore Me? Are the distractions so great that they have taken My place? The enemy deceives you and you follow. I am here, waiting for you patiently. Come back to Me, My children. Follow My ways and be blessed. Grace abounds in My presence. Love is here. Provision is here. Abundance is here. Everything you need is here. Why are you not here? Will you leave your brother behind and follow Me?

Fourth, be ready to leave at a moment's notice. Be prepared to remain close or go far to a distant land. Money will mean nothing. Wealth will be defined differently so prepare yourselves.

Don't get caught unprepared, as it could mean death. Let go of your worldly possessions, for they mean nothing to Me. If they mean nothing to Me, why do they mean so much to you? Define yourself in Me and not in the world. If I asked you to sell your car, would you do it? Would you sell your land? Your jewelry? What you deem as valuable, others will not. What you deem as not valuable, other will value. Keep only those things. Discard the rest.

War will hit America. My people must be prepared. It will be like nothing you can imagine. It will shock the world but there will be little sympathy and less assistance. Most countries will not have the means to help. The dollar will fail. But have no fear. I wil l be with you all. I will be with you always. The end of time has not yet come so prepare yourselves.

No one is listening. They do not want to believe that America is not safe. But I am speaking to My Prophets. At the appointed time, they will speak out in unison. The melody will rise up like a fragrance to My nostrils. It will ring true in everyone's ear and there will be action. My people will respond in one accord. There will be harmony in the Kingdom. The world will look and wonder and the enemy will be confused. What a glorious day in the midst of chaos.

And then America will be rebuilt. Like the original settlers all will be new. I will bless My people abundantly. There will be a new Promised Land!

Suppressed technology will emerge. A new ecology will be in place. My people will live life on a whole different level. What used to be futuristic will be common place. Economic rules will change. Man will no longer dictate seed time and harvest.

There will be a new world order but My people will not be

subject to it. Be wise and vigilant as I will know My people by their spirit. I will judge their hearts. Those who do not belong to Me will be a part of the world order and they are not to be trusted. That world belongs to the enemy.

Enough time has passed for people to have chosen to be one of Mine. Now, I will choose. They must choose life in Me or death by the new world order.

Your currency will be no more. What wealth will you have without the dollar? You must plan now. Sit with Me and I will give you specific instructions.

People in high places already know what is coming and are preparing themselves. But I want My people prepared. The people in high places do not know My heart. My people will know My heart and will be more prepared. No one will be prepared like My people.

This is how they know that I am real. The whole world will know that I exist and yet they will still reject Me. They will say 'He is Jehovah but I am my own god. I do not worship Him but I worship myself.' And I will cry out and strike them and afflict them for their insolence.

But My people will be free of disease. In their quiet time, I will instruct them in how to eat and take care of their bodies. The obedient ones will thrive. My people will be protected from the worldly plights.

VISION GIVEN ON OCTOBER 21, 2006

While praying, the Lord lifted me up high above the earth where clouds float. When I looked down, I could see North America. The United States and Canada were clear and colorful like on a world globe. Then He said "Look daughter, see the destruction that will come?" And I saw billows of smoke all across America, even in Canada. But it did not cover the entire continent. The smoke bellows were spaced out. You could see some land that was not touched by smoke. But I knew there was destruction in every one of the smoke bellows. Then I saw men rising up out of the smoke. They were soldiers, but not American. They were marching across the land gathering up people.

Then the Lord said *"This is why I want My people prepared. This is what is coming."* And I opened my eyes and stopped the vision because I was afraid of what I saw; so much so, that I did not pray for two days.

CHAPTER 1

FEAR NOT!

"Courage is knowing what not to fear."

Plato

While researching and writing *The Bridge*, I had to keep telling myself to fear not as I was coming across startling but accurate information concerning the topics presented in this book. Generally, how the Lord deals with me concerning these types of prophecies is that He will tell me or show me, and then I search out 'proof' in the natural of what He said is to come. I tell you this because I believe what God has revealed is about to take place. And yet, God tells us ahead of time, so that we can prepare and not be anxious or live in fear. The stark reality of these words and visions still startles me. I sometimes hope these events will not come true. But all that I've confirmed in the natural about God's revelations have either happened, or are starting to happen. There are going to be major shifts all around the world.

It is difficult not to feel anxious and fearful for what I've written in these pages. But this information is not intended to put the reader in a state of paralyzing fear. God is <u>with us</u> even through tough times. Know that our God will <u>never</u> leave us or forsake us.[11] In Joshua 1 we are commanded to be strong and courageous:

> *"Be strong and of good courage, for to this people you shall divide as an inheritance the land which I swore to their fathers to give them. Only be strong and very courageous that you may observe to do according to all the law which Moses My servant commanded you; do not turn from it to the right hand or to the left, that you may prosper wherever you go."*
>
> Joshua 1:6-7 (NKJV)

The information contained here is meant to provide peace to the reader by presenting a comprehensive understanding of what has happened, how those patterns can determine what will happen, and by offering specific strategies about how to prepare ourselves, our families and our spheres of influence, so that we can all survive and be at peace even in times of economic turmoil.

This is **not** a time for fear, but for Faith; faith that God will see you through every hour of every day **if** you trust Him. Fear of the unknown creates panic. But this book reveals what is not common knowledge so that those who belong to God can cast off fear, stand in faith before God, and prepare for what's coming. *The Bridge*

---

[11] Deuteronomy 31:6 and Hebrews 13:5 (NKJV).

seeks to build your faith in God through knowledge sharing, despite increasing turmoil in the financial realm. Keep your focus on God and you will weather the coming economic storm.

The phrases "do not be afraid" and "fear not" occur hundreds of times in the Bible. The following are a few examples:

> *"Look, the Lord your God has set the land before you; go up and possess it, as the Lord God of your fathers has spoken to you; **do not fear** or be discouraged."*
>
> Deuteronomy 1:21 (NKJV)

> *"For I, the Lord your God, will hold your right hand, saying '**Fear not**, I will help you.'"*
>
> Isaiah 41:13 (NKJV)

> *"There is no fear in love; but perfect love casts out fear, because fear involves torment. But he who fears has not been made perfect in love."*
>
> 1 John 4:18 (NKJV)

Our Heavenly Father wants us to understand that He is more than capable of taking care of all our needs, including our financial security. Whatever we face, we are to trust Him and fear not.

As the God of Abraham, Isaac, and Jacob encouraged His beloved called, chosen, and covenanted patriarchs, He continues to encourage and remind His chosen covenant people today. For we are Abraham's seed, according to

Galatians 3:29 (NKJV) – "If you are Christ's, then you are Abraham's seed, and heirs according to the promise."

Do not be afraid of what you see happening in the world. Trust in God. He will provide for you.

> *"I will lift up my eyes to the hills – From whence comes my help? My help comes from the LORD, Who made heaven and earth. He will not allow your foot to be moved; He who keeps you will not slumber. Behold, He who keeps Israel shall neither slumber nor sleep. The LORD is your keeper; The LORD is your shade at your right hand. The sun shall not strike you by day, nor the moon by night. The LORD shall preserve you from all evil; He shall preserve your soul. The LORD shall preserve your going out and your coming in from this time forth, and even forevermore."*

Psalm 121:1-8 (NKJV)

The children of Israel had been physically enslaved for so long (400 years) that it took a whole generation to get them completely delivered from mental bondage. That must not happen to those who belong to God today. The transition process from the old economic system to the new may take a period of several years. But during that time, wealth will be transferred from the world, to God's chosen people, specifically for the rebuilding of America, and for the establishment of God's Kingdom on the earth.

Believers are called to impart God's manifold wisdom into the earth. Strategies within this book provide one approach from among many options. Yet, *The Bridge* does provide specific action steps that God's children can take. The coming economic storm has been allowed by God and it will run its course. The Body of Christ needs to prepare for it. In Genesis 41:32 (NKJV), Joseph told Egypt's Pharaoh, "Why was the dream doubled for Pharaoh? Because the thing is established by God, and God will shortly bring it to pass."

The Bridge is **not** meant to instill fear in order to sell books or currency kits. We refuse to cater to or prey on people's fears regarding economic uncertainty. Neither is this a get rich quick scheme. Rather, it is a means of preparation for those chosen and called by God to undertake the strategies herein.

> *"You, children, are from God and have overcome the false prophets, because he who is in you is greater than he who is in the world. They are from the world; therefore, they speak from the world's viewpoint; and the world listens to them. We are from God. Whoever knows God listens to us; whoever is not from God doesn't listen to us. This is how we distinguish the Spirit of truth from the spirit of error. Also we have come to know and trust the love that God has for us. God is love; and those who remain in this love remain united with God, and God remains united with them.*
>
> *This is how love has been brought to maturity with us: as the Messiah is, so are we in the world. This gives us confidence for the Day of Judgment. There is no fear in love. On the contrary, love that*

has achieved its goal gets rid of fear, because fear has to do with punishment; the person who keeps fearing has not been brought to maturity in regard to love. We ourselves love now because He loved us first."

1 John 4:4-6, 16-19 (NKJV)

This book's purpose is to equip God's holy, called, and chosen people for what God is about to allow in the earth.

CHAPTER 2

America's Looming Financial Transition

> *"I mean to tear apart the current system. A Kingdom system will be put into place. That all economic systems will be Kingdom-based is not likely, for the fullness of time has not yet been completed. ... But My system of operation will be key and vital to all other systems."*
>
> Word from the Lord, August 2018

In the fall of 2006, the Lord showed me that in the future, the United States will barter for goods and services for a short period of time. He said, *"What we see as valuable today will have no value during this time and what we perceive as having no value today will have great value for trading while we are in this temporary system."* Why will we barter? The reason is we will not have access to the money that sits in our bank accounts.

How can this be? We are told regularly by the mainstream media that our economy is strong, that our banking system is strong. It is not conceivable to most of us when we put our hard-earned money in the banks that we will not have the ability to access it whenever we want. When given this word, I was not sure how these things were going to happen. Then, the 2008 financial crisis hit the U.S., and many banks on unstable financial ground went under. After this time, the Lord began to explain to me that what happened in 2008 <u>will</u> happen again. But, the next time, it will be much, much worse!

The intention of this book is to bring to light what is about to happen to the world economy. My hope is to provide enough information for people to take action in their personal lives and prepare for what is going to happen.

First, I want to explain how I believe the next financial crisis will happen based on what the Lord showed me. Then I will provide examples of what limited money in the banking system will look like based on both what happened in the past, as well as what is currently happening in other countries. Finally, I will suggest strategies for individual survival during the economic crisis that is coming to America. These strategies may also help those who have ears to hear to potentially take part in the wealth transfer I believe the Lord said is coming.

"To the person who pleases Him God gives wisdom, knowledge and happiness, but to the sinner He gives the task of gathering and storing up wealth to hand it over to the one who pleases God."

Ecclesiastes 2:26

CHAPTER 3

What will Happen with the Banks?

> *"The banks will fail again. But this time, there will not be a quick fix. There will be a period of time before the banking system rights itself again. By then, there will be multiple ways of transacting business in the marketplace. Never again will so few people have control over the worlds' economy."*
>
> Word from the Lord, June 2018

As I mentioned before, in the fall of 2006, while praying, the Lord showed me that at some point in the future, the American people will need to barter for goods and services for a short period of time. Why will bartering become necessary? The reason is because during this period, either we will not have access to our bank accounts or the dollar value will be almost worthless, having lost significant purchasing power in the looming economic collapse. Or, both events may happen.

One factor that will trigger the coming American banking shutdown is a financial product called derivatives. Currently, banks around the world are heavily investing in this volatile financial instrument.[12] Bank investments in derivative contracts have increased significantly since the 2008 mortgage crisis. But back then, mortgage-backed securities were the types of derivatives that caused the 2008 financial crisis. Derivatives are explained more specifically in Chapter 4.

In 1973, David Wilkerson (1931-2011), an evangelist and prophet who founded World Challenge, Inc. in Lindale, Texas, received a prophecy concerning a worldwide banking collapse. The following is an excerpt from that prophecy:

"It is just about to happen very soon; and I am speaking prophetically. If I've ever heard anything from God in my life I heard it! About the nations! Poland owes $30 Billion and they haven't even paid the interest in two years! Saudi Arabia is behind on their payments on $8 Billion – the richest country in the world as far as Arab states and it is not paying its bills! Very soon a European or North African or Eastern nation is going to default on its international loan and when that happens within two weeks Mexico is going to default. Mexico owes $100 Billion – 80% of it to American banks – and here is what is going to happen: About two weeks after the first country goes bankrupt we are going to survive that because most of that money is owed to European banks; German, Swiss and French banks.

"The 2nd country is going to go down probably Argentina or Brazil and we will kind of live that out and people will settle down and say "Well maybe it's not going to hurt." But two weeks after the first country goes down, Mexico is going to default on $100 Billion. And when the banks open the next day at 9:00 am in the morning

---

12 Editors, OTC Derivatives Outstanding, *Bank for International Settlements*, December 16, 2018. http://www.bis.org/statistics/derstats.htm (accessed November 18, 2018).

What will Happen with the Banks?

$15 Billion an hour is going to be withdrawn from our American banks. They are going to be running our banks; the Arabs, all the Latin American countries. They are going to be running our banks – and before the day is over the United States is going to have to declare a bank holiday. And we are going into six months of the worst hell America has ever seen! There is going to be chaos! Not even the National Guard is going to be able to quiet it down. We are going to have to call out the whole United States Army."

"Now I've had visions recently for I've been in New York City and I was in Macy's in a vision and I saw people walking around stunned because they couldn't get their money out the bank. Now I'm going to give you a word of advice. The first country that goes bankrupt, and I've documented this and I've got it sealed in an envelope and I'm going to call all my friends and I'm telling you – this is the first time I've said it in a public meeting like this – but the first country that bellies up you get every dime you have – church get your money out of the bank because you've got two weeks because there's going to be a bank holiday and you won't be able to get a dime for six months. Now of course, there is going to be order restored, but the nation will never be like it is again. There is going to be fear like we've never known. Judgment is at the door!"[13]

I believe the derivatives market will be a catalyst for a worldwide run on America's banks, causing them to crash once again. I also believe it is possible that this approaching nationwide bank failure could result in the imposition of Martial Law across America. Many prophets including Dr. Patricia Green,[14]

---

13 David Wilkerson, "David Wilkerson's Prophecy of Run on Americas Banks," ed. Don Koenig, The Prophetic Years, September 18, 2007. https://www.thepropheticyears.com/wordpress/david-wilkersons-prophecy-of-run-on-american-banks-by-david-wilderson.html (accessed January 21, 2018).
14 Sher Zieve, "A Woman of Faith and Prophetic Warnings," Renew America, July 15, 2015.

David Phillips[15] and Apostle Barbara R. Thomas,[16] have foretold this series of events.

During the 1929 stock market crash, the run on the banks was primarily carried out by individual account holders. When the next run on U.S. banks happens, it will be perpetrated by foreign governments and individual foreign investors. These entities and investors will pull money out of American banks at record speed. However, they will not enter through the front doors of brick and mortar banks to withdraw the money. Their method of withdrawals won't be visibly obvious, so the average American won't be aware of what is happening until it is too late.

HOW THE DRAMA MAY PLAY OUT

As of this writing, a run on the banks will probably look a lot different than what Wilkerson described way back in 1973. Banking transactions today are most often done electronically. Many people receive paychecks as direct deposits and pay their bills electronically. In this day and age, not many people have to go to a physical bank to gain access to their funds. If international customers, including banks want to withdraw their funds from an American bank, some kind of electronic transfer is initiated. Thus, a run on the banks today can happen electronically whereby very large sums of money are withdrawn and as I stated previously, the general public would have no idea it was happening.

---

http://www.renewamerica.com/columns/zieve/150715 (accessed December 30, 2018).
15 David Phillips, "Living with Martial Law," Prophecy Club, April 19, 2016. http://www.prophecyclub.com/latest-prophecies/-living-with-martial-law (accessed December 30, 2018).
16 Apostle Barbara Thomas, "America: We're in Preparation for Martial Law!" His Kingdom Prophecy, November 25, 2018. https://www.hiskingdomprophecy.com/america-were-in-preparation-for-marshall-law/ (accessed December 30, 2018).

What will Happen with the Banks?

A bank holiday could come in the form of a "system error" whereby a banking customer would not have the ability to withdraw money from an ATM machine. The merchant card machines at the store could suddenly "malfunction" and the store would then require cash for purchases. The credit card function on the gas pump could stop working and cash would then be required for gas purchases. When all these things happen, most people will think it is temporary and will only last for a few hours. Some will head to the bank to withdraw cash. You will be able to go into your local branch and see a teller to withdraw money at least in the first day or two until cash at local banks runs out. After that, the banks will likely close their doors. Electronic transactions such as wiring money will still happen, like at a Western Union where actual cash is collected up front for the transfer.

The majority of this run on America's banks may happen over a weekend. ATM's could give out money until each ATM machine runs out of cash. When that happens, there will likely not be any cash to refill the machines. Some significant indicators that America's banks have run out of cash will overlap and span several days before anyone is aware that there is a fundamental problem. In the beginning, it will seem like a minor inconvenience in our normal, everyday access to electronic transactions and computers; a glitch in the system that will be worked out quickly. To make matters worse, the mainstream news media will spin these no-access-to-cash issues as glitches; all to avoid public panic for as long as possible. Eventually, some banks will re-open. But they will impose strict limits on how much money account holders can withdraw.

The 2008 bank failure provoked changes to finance laws.

Thus, contingency plans have been put into place to protect the taxpayer. The Dodd-Frank Wall Street Reform and Consumer Protection Act of 2010 gave the Federal Deposit Insurance Corporation ("FDIC") broader powers to make decisions concerning banks in default. However, Title II, Section 210 of the Dodd-Frank law also legalized derivative contracts which made them legally binding. So these contracts must be honored whether as a loss or a gain regardless of a banks' solvency.[17]

This means that if American banks hold derivative contracts at a loss, by law they have to pay them using any available assets, even if that causes the bank to fail.[18] These derivative contracts are FDIC-insured. Our personal accounts are also FDIC-insured. But there are not enough funds in the insurance accounts of banks to pay both account holders' deposits and losing derivative contracts if a large scale failure happens all at once.

When a bank is about to fail, the FDIC steps in and sells the bank's assets to an existing stronger bank. Many have seen this happen repeatedly over the years. For example, Washington Mutual Bank purchased by JP Morgan Chase Bank in September 2008, and PFF Bank & Trust was purchased by U.S. Bank in November of the same year.[19] When this happens, the strain on the Deposit Insurance Fund (DIF) is minimal. Generally, bank failures happen to smaller banks first. But imagine larger banks failing, too. Who will purchase bank assets then? As of June 2019 in America, banks

---

17 Chris Dodd and Barney Frank, "The Dodd-Frank Wall Street Reform and Consumer Protection Act," Pub.L. 111-203, H.R. 4173 (2010), § 210(a)(H). https://www.congress.gov/bill/111th-congress/house-bill/4173/text (accessed February 16, 2019).
18 Ibid.
19 Editors, "Failing Bank List," Federal Deposit Insurance Corporation, updated February 1, 2019. https://www.fdic.gov/bank/individual/failed/banklist.html (accessed February 16, 2019).

hold $14.7 billion[20] in deposits from individual account holders.

Let's look at a few facts to give us a better understanding of the prophetic word the Lord showed me and why I believe the U.S. banking system is in trouble.

As of June 2019, the Deposit Insurance Fund ("DIF") holds $107.4 billion.[21] This amount is meant to cover the $14.7 billion in individual account holder bank deposits that are insured by the FDIC. On paper, this amount is more than enough to cover individuals' deposits. But when you factor in the $204.9 trillion in derivative contracts held by the banks as of June 30, 2019[22], $107.4 billion is not enough to cover potential losses to the American people.

Normally, it would be unthinkable for a crisis so large to happen that the DIF would be at all strained when trying to reimburse account holders. But, add the $14.7 billion from individuals to the $204.9 trillion in derivative contracts' exposure. Even if only a fraction of these derivative contracts were required to be covered by the FDIC, the DIF will not likely have enough cash. In the event that the FDIC runs out of money trying to cover both losing derivative contracts and individual account holder deposits, they may decide to print more money. However, if they do, inflation will increase to the point that hyperinflation will ensue.

---

20 Editors, "Quarterly Banking Profile, Second Quarter 2019," *Federal Deposit Insurance Corporation*, August 2019, p. 6. https://www.fdic.gov/bank/analytical/qbp/2019jun/qbp.pdf (accessed September 19, 2019).
21 Bret Edwards, "CFO Report – Second Quarter 2019," *Federal Deposit Insurance Corporation*, August , 30, 2019, https://www.fdic.gov/about/strategic/corporate/cfo-report-2ndqtr-19/0619-cfo-report.pdf (accessed September 24, 2019).
22 Editors, "Quarterly Report on Bank Trading and Derivatives Activities," September, 2019, Table 1, *Office of the Comptroller of the Currency*, https://www.occ.gov/publications-and-resources/publications/quarterly-report-on-bank-trading-and-derivatives-activities/files/q2-2019-derivatives-quarterly.html, (accessed October 1, 2019).

To stem inflation, the Federal Reserve may reduce interest rates, but as of September 20, 2019, the current interest rate is only 1.90%.[23] How much lower can it go? Another option would be for the Federal Reserve to move to a negative interest rate. Doing so might mean that individual bank customers would pay a fee to take money out of their own accounts.

I believe that the hypothetical scenario just described will, if it happens, cause America's banks to close their doors. This is not intended to scare anyone, but to inform in order to help you get educated and prepare. This knowledge is necessary so that the reader understands how serious the situation can become. If banks close their doors and block access to your funds, then you will also be unable to use your ATM or debit card. This means purchasing everyday items, such as groceries and gas, will require cash. Having cash on hand is going to be very important, at least in the short term.

---

23 Editors, "Federal Fund Rate-Historical Annual Yield Data," *Macro Trends*, updated September 20, 2019. https://www.macrotrends.net/2015/fed-funds-rate-historical-chart, (accessed September 24, 2019).

CHAPTER 4

What is a Derivative?

> *"Derivatives are financial weapons of mass destruction, carrying dangers that, while now latent, are potentially lethal."*
>
> Warren Buffet[24]

Derivatives are very complex financial products. But rather than providing a simplified definition, I will first present an overview, and then describe these instruments in specific detail to help the reader gain a basic understanding of what is an extremely convoluted subject.

DERIVATIVES IN SIMPLE TERMS

A derivative is a speculation between parties regarding how an asset will perform in the future. For example, I can speculate or bet that in one month's time, the price of oil will increase by $5 per barrel. You can bet against me. Other assets we can bet on include interest rates, exchange rates between different currencies, the price of wheat, the value of crypto currencies like Bitcoins, and mortgages. It is important to note that there is something of value, an asset, about which we are

---

[24] Warren Buffet, "Letter to Shareholders," *Berkshire Hathaway*, February 21, 2003, p. 15. http://www.berkshirehathaway.com/letters/2002pdf.pdf (accessed January 22, 2019).

betting. The purpose of the asset is to make the bet secure. To understand how complicated derivatives can become, I have created four terms to describe their possible progression: Original Derivative ("OD"), Secondary Derivative ("SD"), Messy Derivative ("MD"), and Very Messy Derivative ("VMD").

Original Derivative – The original derivative contract or speculation on an asset or assets.

Secondary Derivative – We place 10 ODs for interest rates into a bowl. Then, we stir the ODs to mix all the interest rate values together as if mixing cake batter. Next, we divide the value into 12 or more parts and sell off each piece to various investment agencies at wholesale prices. These investment agencies sell each piece to individual or group investors; like your 401(k), pension funds and mutual funds.

Messy Derivative – Grab several ODs with a combination of different underlying assets and put them in a pot. Let's say we use one oil OD, three wheat ODs, two foreign currency ODs, the interest rate SD mentioned above, and 13 mortgages. We mix these contracts up and then divide the mixture 50 ways and sell off each piece.

Very Messy Derivative – This is the result of the repeated combining, splitting, and selling of SDs and MDs, all over the world. Pension funds, 401(k) funds, and mutual funds have all likely purchased derivatives as part of their investment.

DERIVATIVES: A FINANCIAL DEFINITION

A derivative is a financial contract (like the OD and SD examples listed above) in which the value is derived from the performance of underlying market factors, such as interest rates, currency exchange rates, and stock price.[25] A derivative contract can contain futures,[26] options,[27] debt obligations,[28] deposits, and/or varying combinations of other security contracts. The derivative's value fluctuates based upon the underlying assets' fluctuating value.[29]

Derivatives can also get their value from an asset purchase in which the agreement between a buyer and seller predicts how much the asset price will change within a specified time period. The underlying asset of the derivative contract can be oil, gold, agriculture, energy products, stocks, bonds, or currencies, including the U.S. dollar.

For example, if oil currently trades at $48 dollars per barrel, a contract could be created to predict that two days from now, oil will trade at $50 per barrel. The buyer can either purchase the option to agree that the price will increase to $50 per barrel, or the option to disagree. At the end of two days, if the price of oil is any amount less than $50 per barrel, the person who initially agreed that the price would go up to $50 has to pay the price difference to the person who disagreed. If the price of oil is more than $50 per barrel (say $55) then the person who agreed that the price would increase gets paid $5 by the person who disagreed.

The above is a very simplistic example to illustrate how a derivative contract might work. There are a variety of derivative contracts that contain varying terms. The buyer enters into a

---

25 James Chen, "What is a 'Derivative,'" *Investopedia*, Updated June 25, 2019. https://www.investopedia.com/ask/answers/12/derivative.asp (accessed September 24, 2019).
26 Futures are contracts to purchase or sell a specific financial instrument at a future date and price.
27 Options are a buyer's right, but not obligation, to buy or sell a financial instrument at a specific price on a specific date.
28 A debt obligation is an asset-backed security. (A security is a guarantee to repay a loan.)
29 Jean Folger, "What is a 'Derivative,'" Investopedia, November 1, 2017. https://www.investopedia.com/ask/answers/12/derivative.asp (accessed January 22, 2018).

contract by disagreeing with the seller, which means there will always be a winner and a loser in these transactions. If the price does increase to $50 per barrel, then they both may win but the amount will be less for both parties. However, the one who wrote the contract (the seller) will generally receive a commission for the contract regardless if the contract wins, loses, or breaks even.

Another example is a derivative based on bond interest rates. A contract could predict that a bond's current interest rate will remain at the stated price when the bond comes to maturity, or that the interest rate will adjust up or down. A buyer could predict that the interest rate will remain constant, decrease by a specific amount, or increase by a specific amount. If the buyer predicts that the interest rate will decrease at the time of bond maturity, and the bond price does not decrease but remains constant, then the buyer owes the difference between the initial rate and the predicted decreased rate to the seller. The same holds true, if the buyer predicts an interest rate increase, and it stays constant. Here, again, the buyer would owe the difference to the seller.

Banks make a lot of money on derivative contracts. In the third quarter of 2018 alone, American banks made $7.1 billion in trading revenue,[30] compared to $6.4 billion in the third quarter of 2016.[31] On the surface, these profits make derivatives contracts seem like they are worth the risk. While the Dodd-Frank law attempts to regulate derivative contracts,

---

30 Editors, "Quarterly Report on Bank Trading and Derivatives Activities, Third Quarter 2018," Office of the Comptroller of the Currency, December 2018, p. 3. https://www.occ.gov/topics/capital-markets/financial-markets/derivatives/pub-derivatives-quarterly-qtr3-2018.pdf (accessed December 30, 2018).

31 Editors, "Quarterly Report on Bank Trading and Derivatives Activities, Third Quarter 2016," Office of the Comptroller of the Currency, January 2017, p. 3. https://www.occ.gov/topics/capital-markets/financial-markets/derivatives/pub-derivatives-quarterly-qtr3-2016.pdf (accessed December 30, 2018).

What is a Derivative?

oversight is difficult because these contracts are very complex; often including multiple and various underlying assets. The complexity of the contracts makes it difficult to determine the actual risks associated with each derivative product. Banks are allowed by law to balance their exposure to risk by balancing their derivative assets against their liabilities.[32] In other words, banks are allowed to focus on the worth of the products rather than the costs associated with them. The problem with this approach is that derivatives are already a form of debt. Standard accounting procedures allow derivatives to be classified as assets **if** the fair value of derivative returns is deemed positive and there is an accounting policy in place within that contract.[33]

A layman's comparison would be a house with a mortgage. The house is considered an asset, but it's not really an asset because of the mortgage or liability attached to it. Unless the home is owned free of a mortgage, it is a debt. We saw this first-hand during the 2008 financial crisis. Many people lost their homes. Homeowners thought they were holding an asset but it did not take long for them to realize that their homes were actually liabilities or debt. In fact, subprime mortgage-backed securities are partially to blame for causing the 2008 financial crisis. These securities were a kind of derivative that was heavily invested in by individuals and entities around the world prior to the 2008 crisis.[34]

Berkshire Hathaway CEO Warren Buffett, the third richest man in the world whose net worth is $83.4 billion, said this

---

32 Blaine B, "Netting Derivatives on a Balance Sheet, Can I Do It?" Popular Accounting, August 5, 2015. http://www.popularaccounting.com/2015/08/05/netting-derivatives-on-the-balance-sheet-can-i-do-it/ (accessed November 29, 2018).
33 Ibid., 45-46.
34 Alessandro Bruno, "The 2008 Financial Crisis Explained," Lombardi Letter, May 18, 2017. https://www.lombardiletter.com/the-2008-financial-crisis-explained/11672/ (accessed November 29, 2018).

about derivatives:

"With derivatives, you're exposed to counterparties and thus reliant on others. These claims build up over time to the tune of billions of dollars and when one falls, the whole system falls. Derivatives are not evil by themselves but rather everyone needs to be able to handle them. System wide, they are rat poison."[35]

As of June 2019, American banks hold an estimated $204.9 trillion in derivative contracts.[36] This represents a $15 trillion increase from Second Quarter 2016.[37] Outstanding derivative contracts worldwide currently stand at $595 trillion up from $483 trillion in 2016.[38] The exposure the banks have in relation to derivative contracts puts the entire global banking system at risk of failing. If the banks fail, the American economy as well as the economies in many other countries worldwide will go into chaos. These bank failures will cause a cascade effect in various other segments of our economies. This is what the Lord showed me will happen - all because of banks' irresponsible trading practices in derivative contracts.

DERIVATIVE COLLATERAL

If a derivative contract is an investment, then the underlying asset of that contract is meant to serve as collateral in case that contract fails. American bank assets currently total $16.5 billion, about eight percent of the total amount of their derivative

---

35 Editors, "Warren Buffet Real Time Net Worth," Forbes, January 27, 2019. https://www.forbes.com/profile/warren-buffett/#75e04abf4639 (accessed January 27, 2019).
36 Editors, "Second Quarter Report, 2019," 10.
37 Editors, "Second Quarter Report, 2016," 14.
38 Editors, "Statistical release: OTC derivatives statistics at end-December 2019", Bank of International Settlements, May 2, 2019, p. 1. https://www.bis.org/publ/otc_hy1905.pdf (accessed October 2, 2019).

exposure.³⁹ If the derivative market fails again, as it did in 2008, banks will not have enough assets to pay their debts. This situation is why the federal government bailed out American banks in 2008. It is also why the body of Christ needs to prepare now for what's coming, using strategies such as the Currency Kit, which will be explained in Chapter 12. People will need to store up necessities before America's banks fail again. In this way, readers will minimize the effects of the impending economic collapse.

The 2010 Dodd Frank Act was passed to prevent the Federal Reserve from intervening in any future financial crises by using taxpayer funds to pay for bank bailouts.⁴⁰ Covering bank losses is now the responsibility of the FDIC. The Federal Reserve is the central bank of the United States and controls monetary policies for the country. The FDIC insures our banks and thrifts in case of failure.

After the 2008 financial crisis, the Holy Spirit revealed to me that eventually, the derivatives market will crash, and crash hard. These derivative liabilities will then become a catalyst for a global banking shutdown. Some banks will do so temporarily; for others, these closures will be permanent. Such shutdowns will cut off Americans' access to their own bank accounts for a short period of time, but possibly for up to six months or longer. In order to adjust to this sudden financial scarcity, I believe a bartering system will develop for the exchange of goods and services.

While writing this book, I asked the Lord for a timeline

---

39 Editors, "Quarterly Report on Bank Trading and Derivatives Activities, Third Quarter 2018, Table 1," Office of the Comptroller of the Currency, December 2018. https://www.occ.gov/topics/capital-markets/financial-markets/derivatives/pub-derivatives-quarterly-qtr3-2018.pdf (January 23, 2019).
40 Dodd and Frank, "The Dodd Frank Wall Street Reform Act."

of when we can expect to see the failure of America's larger banks and the subsequent full collapse of the U.S. economy. On September 30, 2018, God told me that it would be 3 or 4 years. This sets the approximate timeframe for the approaching failure of banks worldwide at sometime between 2021 and 2022.

Lynette Zang, Chief Market Analyst with ITM Trading predicts a possible global collapse of banks to happen in 2021.[41] Her reason: in April 2018, the Federal Reserve changed their interest rate protocol from the London Interbank Offered Rate (LIBOR) to the Secured Overnight Financing Rate (SOFR). The discontinuation of the LIBOR standard, a benchmark representing rates that banks offer each other for short-term loans, is the result of a lack of a confidence because of the rate manipulations during the 2008 financial crisis. As a result of this change by the Fed, bank regulators around the world have pushed to find alternatives to LIBOR as well.[42]

According to Zang, language concerning the change from LIBOR to SOFR must be either inserted into existing contracts or the contracts themselves must be re-written. However, 95% of current contracts tied to LIBOR are "highly complex derivative contracts that require 100% agreement among thousands of investors."[43] Zang believes this will make the transition of existing contracts from LIBOR to SOFR a challenge. Zang also believes such a transition will change the value of the underlying contracts, which could have a domino effect on valuations for both the

---

41 Lynette Zang, "Entering the Minefield: Is Your Armor Ready?" ITM Trading, November 28, 2018. https://www.itmtrading.com/blog/entering-minefield-armor-ready-lynette-zang/ (accessed December 9, 2018).
42 Karen Brettell, "What is SOFR? The New U.S. Libor Alternative," Reuters, April 3, 2018. https://www.reuters.com/article/us-usa-bonds-sofr-explainer/what-is-sofr-the-new-u-s-libor-alternative-idUSKCN1HA0H1 (accessed December 9, 2018).
43 Zang, "Entering the Minefield."

What is a Derivative?

derivative contracts and the banks and corporations who purchased or sold them.[44] So, if the transition from LIBOR to SOFR takes place around the world, the derivative contracts held by banks in countries where this change is implemented could be completely devalued overnight, or in the very least, run huge debt margins.

Part of the problem with the LIBOR standard is that the interest rates are based on subjective judgment; what the bank executives think the rates should be. As a result, LIBOR contracts are potentially grossly overvalued. By sharp contrast, SOFR comprises four characteristics, the primary one being that it is fully transaction-based. Combined with the other characteristics (encompasses a robust underlying market, overnight nearly risk-free reference rate, and covers multiple repo market segments), SOFR rates are market-driven and are supposed to better represent loan rates based on a more accurate picture of valuation.[45] The change from the LIBOR to the SOFR standard is supposed to eliminate or minimize interest rate manipulation by making sure rates are more closely aligned with the market.

That being said, over $200 trillion in derivative contracts and loans are currently using the LIBOR standard. And derivatives account for 95% of these outstanding contracts.[46] A future resetting of the rates for these contracts based on a transition from LIBOR to SOFR may be part of why the banks are going to collapse. Because these contracts are so deeply interconnected, it would only take the failure of a few large banks after a timely transition from LIBOR to SOFR, to cause the collapse of many,

---
44 Ibid.
45 Joshua Frost, "Introducing the Secured Overnight Financing Rate (SOFR)," Federal Reserve Bank of New York, November 2, 2017. https://www.newyorkfed.org/medialibrary/media/newsevents/speeches/2017/Frostpresentation.pdf (accessed December 9, 2018).
46 Brettell, "What is SOFR?"

many more. According to Zang, a <u>best</u>-case scenario for such a transition will still cause a major shake-up in the markets.

DID CONGRESS REALLY PROTECT US FROM ANOTHER BANK CRISIS?

In 2015, the Lord instructed me to focus on learning more about America's banking system. Among other things, I was prompted to read the 2010 Dodd Frank Act, which was created in response to the 2008 financial crisis.[47] The Dodd Frank Act broadened the FDIC's power over depository institutions under their jurisdiction. The law's primary purpose is to prevent Congress from ever again using taxpayer money for bank bailouts. In theory, increasing the FDIC's power in this way should protect taxpayer funds. The law provides further protection by increasing deposit insurance from $100,000 to $250,000 for each account holder.[48] The purpose of the law is "to end 'too big to fail,' to protect the American taxpayer by ending bailouts, to protect consumers from abusive financial services practices, and for other purposes."[49] However, I believe Dodd Frank has <u>not</u> fixed the underlying problem because it has not curbed the banks' risky derivative investment practices. The law merely shifted decision-making powers regarding how to handle bank failures and bailouts from the Federal Reserve to the FDIC. In doing so, it transferred responsibility and authority to decide what to do if another financial crisis happens from Congress to an independent federal agency, not accountable to We, the American People.

Since the early part of this century, banks have been taking

---

[47] Dodd and Frank, "The Dodd-Frank Wall Street Reform Act."
[48] U.S. Congress, "Federal Deposit Insurance Act," 12 U.S.C. 1821(a)(1)(E), Cornell School of Law, January 7, 2011. https://www.law.cornell.edu/uscode/text/12/1821 (accessed November 19, 2018).
[49] Dodd and Frank, "The Dodd Frank Wall Street Reform Act."

extreme risks in the global financial market. As a result, I believe events such as the above-mentioned change from LIBOR to SOFR will lead to banks' inability to fulfill their financial obligations. Over time, this will render many banks insolvent, leading to shutdowns, possibly for several months. Banks in countries such as Greece, Zimbabwe, and more recently Venezuela, have already had to shut down for a period of time. When they did, depositors in those countries had either <u>limited</u> or <u>no</u> access to their funds. The history of events in these countries after the banks closed their doors will be reviewed later. For your reference, below is a list of banks and their derivative holdings as of September 2018:

Top Banks	Derivative Liability	Currently-Held Assets
JP Morgan Case Bank	$ 55.7 trillion	$ 2.4 trillion
Citibank NA	52.6 trillion	1.5 trillion
Goldman Sachs	49.2 trillion	.2 trillion
Bank of America NA	22.2 trillion	1.8 trillion
Wells Fargo Bank NA	12.1 trillion	1.7 trillion
HSBC NA	5.5 trillion	.2 trillion
Bank of New York Mellon	1.1 trillion	.3 trillion
U S Bank National ASSN	.5 trillion	.5 trillion
All Other	11.5 trillion	7.9 trillion
Total	**$204.9 trillion**	**$16.5 trillion**[49]

At present, all that I've described so far seems an unlikely and unrealistic prediction. You could say it's something out of a

---

50 Editors, "Quarterly Report on Bank Trading and Derivatives Activities, Second Quarter 2019, Table 1.

doomsday novel if it were not for the fact that it <u>is</u> happening in America, and has <u>already</u> happened recently in other countries around the world. The catalyst for a failing economy and banking system shutdown and subsequent reset may be different for each country, but the devastating results are all too similar around the world. Learning what happened in other countries, can thus serve as a warning for what could potentially happen in the United States.

CHAPTER 5

Hyperinflation – What is It?

> *"Inflation is the one form of taxation that can be imposed without legislation. It is also a form of taxation that is particularly seductive. In its early stages, people find it rather attractive, because the first effects of inflation are expansionary and pleasant. It's like the first drink you take. It's only the next morning that you have a hangover."*
>
> Milton Freidman[51]

As I stated previously, one catalyst for the coming economic collapse will be banks' inability to pay their derivative contracts. While the reasons that other countries' banking systems fail will differ, the common thread will be hyperinflation. This will lead to the collapse of each nation's currency. By studying previous national economic collapses, we can gain understanding about what may transpire in the United States if our banks fail again.

But first, we need to understand inflation and hyperinflation.

---

51 Frances Cairncross, "Inflation v. Civilization; Frances Cairncross Puts Questions to Professor Milton Friedman, Arch-Exponent of Monetarism," The Guardian, September 21, 1974, p. 15 in Robert Leeson and Charles G. Palm (eds.), The Collected Works of Milton Friedman, The Hoover Institution. https://miltonfriedman.hoover.org/friedman_images/Collections/2016c21/Guardian_09_21_1974.pdf (accessed February 1, 2019).

Inflation happens when the prices of goods increase while the value of money decreases.[52] This is something many of us have already experienced. When I was a little girl, I remember purchasing bubble gum for .05 cents. A few decades later, that same piece of gum now costs five cents. Today, residential rentals and housing prices continue to increase, but our purchasing power hasn't necessarily kept up.

Hyperinflation happens when prices increase by at least 50% within one month's time.[53] For example, if a loaf of bread costs $1.49 at the beginning of a month, but within 30 days, that same bread loaf is $2.24, you have experienced hyperinflation. Imagine if the trend continues. At the end of six months, the loaf would cost the consumer $11.34. Yikes!

Two catalysts for hyperinflation that could lead to an economic crisis in America will be 1) if the rest of the world stops using U.S. dollars ("USD") to transact international trade for goods, or 2) if the rest of the world stops using the Petro dollar to purchase oil. If other countries decide to use a different currency, then the amount of USD in the global economic system will expand, forcing the devaluation of the dollar in America.

In the early twentieth century, the British pound was the go-to currency. World War I changed that when Britain had to borrow money from the U.S. and go off the gold standard. Leading up to World War II, the United States had amassed large amounts of gold from other countries in payment for

---

52 Shobhit Seth, "Inflation," Investopedia, January 16, 2019. https://www.investopedia.com/terms/i/inflation.asp (accessed January 27, 2019).
53 Steve H. Hanke and Nicholas Krus, "World Inflations," Cato Institute, August 2012. https://www.cato.org/publications/working-paper/world-hyperinflations (accessed November 23, 2018).

weapons and supplies. By 1944, to manage foreign exchange, delegates from 44 countries decided to switch to the USD instead of gold since the dollar was linked to gold.[54] The USD's usage as the world reserve currency did not change even after America abandoned the gold standard in 1971.[55]

However, the use of the USD as the sole world reserve currency may soon be coming to an end. In the fall of 2018, China launched a pilot program to pay for its oil imports in their own Renminbi (RMB) currency,[56] moving away from trading with USD for the first time since 1944. Russia and India have also started to move away from trading in USD. China and India are looking to not only move away from USD, but they are also working on creating their own digital currencies, to implement a cashless system for trading.[57]

Economist Mark Armstrong asserted that hyperinflation is a rate of inflation from which there is no return. This means that when hyperinflation takes hold, a country will be unable to recover economically due to government factors, such as fiscal mismanagement.[58] But what if the inflation rate

---

54 Richard Best, "How the U.S. Dollar Became the World's Reserve Currency," Investopedia, October 1, 2018. https://www.investopedia.com/articles/forex-currencies/092316/how-us-dollar-became-worlds-reserve-currency.asp (accessed December 30, 2018).
55 Kimberly Amadeo, "History of the Gold Standard," Investopedia, November 7, 2018. https://www.investopedia.com/articles/forex-currencies/092316/how-us-dollar-became-worlds-reserve-currency.asp (accessed December 30, 2018).
56 Sara Hsu, "The Almighty Dollar: Is US Dominance in the Oil Trade Waning as China Begins using RMB for Payment?" Forbes, April 5, 2018. https://www.forbes.com/sites/sarahsu/2018/04/05/the-almighty-dollar-is-us-dominance-in-the-oil-trade-waning-as-china-begins-using-rmb-for-payment/#30aa583"7bc87 (accessed November 23, 2018).
57 Josh Sigurdson and John Sneisen, "Countless Countries are Swapping Out of the U.S. Dollar. Here are the Most Recent Examples," Silver Doctors, January 1, 2019. https://www.silverdoctors.com/headlines/world-news/the-end-of-the-us-dollar-more-countries-swap-out-of-world-reserve-currency/ (accessed January 23, 2019).
58 Mark Armstrong "Hyperinflation Definition," Armstrong Economics, November 21, 2013. https://www.armstrongeconomics.com/uncategorized/hyperinflation-definition/ (accessed November 23, 2018).

is greater than 50 percent? What effects would such severe hyperinflation have on a country's citizens? Hyperinflation to this extreme has happened to approximately 56 countries throughout world history, including France, China, Germany, Poland, and the Congo (Zaire).[59] More recently, it has happened in Venezuela and Zimbabwe. Let's review the effects of hyperinflation on the economies of these two countries.

---

59 Hanke and Krus, "World Hyperinflation," p 12.

CHAPTER 6

Historical Case Studies: Economic Collapse

"The history of paper money is an account of abuse, mismanagement, and financial disaster."

Richard Ebeling[60]

As I was praying about which case studies to use in *The Bridge,* the Lord led me to research the history of Zimbabwe, Venezuela, and Germany regarding hyperinflation and how these countries reacted to their plight. I believe the case studies mentioned within these pages serve as a reminder and a warning for the United States. For example, from 1914-1924, some people in Germany survived and thrived during their economic plight and others did not. From these case studies we can learn not only what happened, but also how to best protect ourselves when similar events begin to unfold in the United States.

ZIMBABWE

Zimbabwe, an African nation formally known as Rhodesia, was a self-sufficient country with production in maize (similar to corn), tobacco, cotton, beef, roses, and sugarcane.[61] Most

---

60 Richard Ebeling, "Monetary Central Planning and the State, Part 29: The Gold Standard in the 19th Century," The Future of Freedom Foundation, May 1, 1999. https://www.fff.org/explore-freedom/article/monetary-central-planning-state-part-29-gold-standard-19th-century/ (accessed February 11, 2019).
61 Samantha Power, "How To Kill A Country: Turning a Breadbasket into a Basket Case

of the farmland was owned by white citizens. The Zimbabwe government and some of its black citizens considered the white owners lingering evidence of their oppression which caused a civil war whereby the black citizens wrestled Zimbabwe from British rule in 1980.

"After the country's reconstitution as Zimbabwe in 1980, whites had to adjust to being an ethnic minority in a country with a black majority government. Although a significant number of whites remained, many white people emigrated in the early-1980s; both in fear for their lives and an uncertain future. Political unrest and the seizure of many white-owned commercial farms resulted in a further exodus of whites commencing in 1999. The 2002 census recorded 46,743 white people living in Zimbabwe. More than 10,000 were elderly and fewer than 9,000 were under the age of 15."[62]

After the new government was established, Zimbabwe's farms were still primarily owned and managed by descendants of white Europeans. Around the year 2000, black squatters began seizing hundreds of white-owned farms. These citizens were encouraged to do so by the new black-majority government, even though the constitution, which authorized these seizures, was voted down in the legislature. As a result, by 2002, there was a food shortage. In May 2002, a land acquisition law allowed more farmland to be taken away from white owners.[63] That same year, in response to Zimbabwe's removal of a European

---

in Ten Easy Steps-the Robert Mugabe Way," The Atlantic, December 2003. https://www.theatlantic.com/magazine/archive/2003/12/how-to-kill-a-country/302845/ (accessed November 23, 2018).

62 Michael Hartnack, "Zimbabwe Census Sees Flight of Whites," Irish Examiner, August 24, 2005. https://web.archive.org/web/20070929111549/http://archives.tcm.ie/irishexaminer/2005/08/24/story662306828.asp (accessed February 3, 2019).

63 Editors, "Zimbabwe Timeline," Zimfield Guide, October 2016. http://zimfieldguide.com/mashonaland-central/zimbabwe-timeline (accessed November 23, 2018).

Union ("EU") election monitoring team, the EU, International Monetary Fund ("IMF"), and the United States imposed sanctions on Zimbabwe and cut off development aid.[64] By 2005, Zimbabwe began experiencing severe hyperinflation due to the land confiscation and possibly corrupt election results, which led other nations to withdraw their investments as well.

This widespread land confiscation put the country into a desperate situation. Black citizens had not only expelled white farmers; but they also expelled the previous landowners' experienced field hands as well. Those who confiscated the land had little or no farming experience to draw upon, and had expelled the only experienced farmers they could have asked. The sanctions imposed against Zimbabwe's government meant these new farm owners were unable to obtain loans for land development. As a result, food output fell by 45 percent.[65] Then, as unemployment rose, a large number of black citizens became homeless.

In an effort to keep the economy going, the Zimbabwe government began printing more money. In 2005, inflation turned into hyperinflation as the prices of goods increased several times each day. Then banks began to limit how much money account holders could withdraw per day to about $50.[66] People began to sell anything they could to survive. By 2009, hyperinflation had made the Zimbabwe dollar worthless. As a result, the currency was slowly abandoned by businesses

---

64 Staff and Agencies, "EU Imposes Sanctions on Zimbabwe," The Guardian, February 18, 2002. https://www.theguardian.com/world/2002/feb/18/zimbabwe (accessed November 23, 2018).
65 Bill Mitchell, "Zimbabwe for Hyperventilators 101," Economic Outlook, July 29, 2009. http://bilbo.economicoutlook.net/blog/?p=3773 (accessed November 23, 2018).
66 Justina Crabtree, "Zimbabwe's Issuing New 'Bond Notes' to Avoid a Cash Crunch," CNBC, November 28, 2016. https://www.cnbc.com/2016/11/28/zimbabwes-issuing-new-bond-notes-to-avoid-a-cash-crunch.html (accessed November 23, 2018).

and street vendors. In order to conduct business, patrons had to use other currencies including the USD, the South African Rand ("ZAR"), the Botswana Pula ("BWP"), the Euro ("EUR"), and the British Pound Sterling ("GBP").[67] In 2015, the government formally phased out the Zimbabwe dollar using a multi-currency system in an attempt to counter hyperinflation.

Over time, the marketplace in Zimbabwe developed other forms of conducting business including electronic transactions and bartering. People became creative, networking with neighboring countries to exchange currency or goods and also relying on relatives to send funds in USD. Some also re-invented themselves taking advantage of entrepreneurial opportunities to make more money as industry and government were not able to keep up with wages. The black market and other forms of underground transactions and businesses rose up to become an integral part of Zimbabwe's economy. Today, the black market is out in the open in Zimbabwe. Individual black market money changers sit on street corners and in parking lots, and the predominant currency there is the USD.

All other world currencies are currently valued by the U.S. Dollar. In 2016, Zimbabwe introduced bond notes as a temporary fix for their currency predicament. The bond note's value is attached to the USD and backed by a U.S.-granted $200 Million African Export Import Bank loan.[68] One problem, however, is that these bond notes cannot be used outside of Zimbabwe. To further complicate matters, Zimbabwe's citizens prefer to transact business

---

67 Editors, "Zimbabwe Abandons its Currency," BBC, January 29, 2009. http://news.bbc.co.uk/2/hi/7859033.stm (accessed November 23, 2018).
68 Bernard Mpofu and Gabriele Steinhauser, "Zimbabwe to Start Issuing Bond Notes on Monday," The Wall Street Journal, November 26, 2016. https://www.wsj.com/articles/zimbabwe-to-start-issuing-bond-notes-1480171833 (accessed February 16, 2019).

Historical Case Studies: Economic Collapse

using the USD, rather than these bond notes. Many businesses even offer discounts on purchases when the USD is used.[69]

Almost all economic transactions in Zimbabwe are in USD, which means their government does not have any control over the currency. Within the next five years, the government will introduce a new Zimbabwe dollar. Their first task, however, is to put economy-stabilizing policies into place.[70] Considering what is going to happen to the U.S. Dollar, Zimbabwe's move to re-establish their own currency backed by gold or another measure is a good idea.

Zimbabwe Update: Zimbabwe began issuing dollar notes in November 2019. Inflation is still problematic and prior to issuing the dollar notes, there was a cash shortage and cash withdrawals were rationed. It is the hope of the government that the introduction of the dollar notes will alleviate the cash shortage and bring stability to the economy. As of the writing of this update, a loaf of bread cost 15 Zimbabwe dollars and a packet of potatoes 100 dollars. Just over a pound of meat costs 160 dollars.[71]

VENEZUELA

Economically speaking, Venezuela was once the richest country in Central America. Venezuela has the largest oil reserves in the world, followed by Saudi Arabia.[72] This being the case, one

---

69 Abdur Rahman, Alfa Shaban with Reuters, "Zimbabwe Introduces Fresh $5 Bond Notes to Ease Cash Crunch," African News, March 2, 2017. http://www.africanews.com/2017/02/03/zimbabwe-introduces-fresh-5-bond-notes-to-ease-cash-crunch/ (accessed November 23, 2018).
70 Staff Reporter, "Zimbabwe Central Bank Chief Talks Up Currency Reforms," The Zimbabwe Mail, June 30, 2018. http://www.thezimbabwemail.com/banking/zimbabwe-central-bank-chief-talks-up-currency-reforms/ (accessed November 23, 2018).
71 DPA, "Zimbabwe's new dollar notes finally hit the streets.", IOL News, November 12, 2019. https://www.iol.co.za/news/africa/zimbabwes-new-dollar-notes-finally-hit-the-streets-37077931 (accessed December 20, 2019).
72 Jessica Dillinger, "The World's Largest Oil Reserves by Country," World Atlas, October 23,

would think that Venezuela would never experience financial trouble and that their people would have plenty of access to food and medical care. But as of this writing, the Venezuelan people are not only starving, but also lacking basic medical care. Over the past 20 years, several factors have contributed to the current situation in Venezuela. However, my focus is on the banks and hyperinflation's effect on people's ability to access goods and services.

Venezuela's economy is shrinking at an alarming rate. The Gross Domestic Product (GDP), which measures a country's economic activity and monetary value in finished goods and services, has been shrinking since 2004. The initial cause was a strike by oil workers from 2002-2003. In response, the government-run oil company fired 18,000 employees. This drastically affected the quality of work of those who remained employed thereby decreasing production output. Making matters worse, in 2003, Venezuela's Gross National Product (GNP) fell by 27 percent.[73] After this strike, the government instituted measures in an attempt to control the falling value of their currency. They established subsidies for food and consumer goods, nationalized other industries such as farming, and placed some controls on imports.

But revenge in the form of violence and murders against those seen as responsible for the strike was rampant by those outspoken against the current government.[74] In 2017,

---

2018. https://www.worldatlas.com/articles/the-world-s-largest-oil-reserves-by-country.html (accessed November 23, 2018).
73 Michael McCaughan, "The Battle of Venezuela," Journal of Latin American Studies 37(2): 409-410, May 2005. https://www.researchgate.net/publication/231843642_Michael_McCaughan_The_Battle_of_Venezuela_London_Latin_America_Bureau_2004_pp_ix166_799_pb (accessed January 27, 2019).
74 Garth Friesen, "The Path to Hyperinflation: What Happened To Venezuela?" Forbes, August 7, 2018. https://www.forbes.com/sites/garthfriesen/2018/08/07/the-path-to-

Historical Case Studies: Economic Collapse

Venezuela's GDP shrank by 16.6 percent.[75] Yet, consumer prices have increased by 46,305% since 2004. That means the current hyperinflation rate is one million percent.[76] What does this look like in real terms? In March 2015, the price of 30 eggs in Venezuela was 1,180 bolivars. Two years later, the same quantity of eggs had increased to 9,600 bolivars.[77] A year and a half after that, the cost of only one dozen eggs had increased to 2.6 million bolivares! However, the same eggs <u>if purchased in USD</u> cost only .60 cents on the black market. Those who are able to obtain USD are faring better than those who only have bolivares with which to purchase food and other necessities.[78]

Venezuela's medical services have also deteriorated. The country has a universal health care system. However, a significant number of the clinics are closed and the hospitals do not have the necessary medical supplies to treat those who arrive for care.[79] In addition, more than half of Venezuela's children have dropped out of school as of 2018. And schools are not able to meet minimum requirements to stay open; 77%

---

hyperinflation-what-happened-to-venezuela/#6edccec915e4 (accessed January 1, 2019).
75 Banco Central De Venezuela, "Venezuela GDP Growth Rate," Trading Economics, December 2018. https://tradingeconomics.com/venezuela/gdp-growth-annual (accessed January 27, 2019).
76 Marco Bello, "IMF Projects Venezuela Inflation will Hit 1,000,000 Percent," Reuters, May 29, 2018. https://www.reuters.com/article/us-venezuela-economy/imf-projects-venezuela-inflation-will-hit-1000000-percent-in-2018-idUSKBN1KD2L9 (accessed November 23, 2018).
77 Stefano Pozzebon and Patrick Gillespie, "Venezuelans are Losing Weight amid Food Shortages, Skyrocketing Prices," CNN Money, May 3, 2017. https://money.cnn.com/2017/05/03/news/economy/venezuela-food-prices/index.html (accessed November 23, 2018).
78 Rachelle Krygier, "In Socialist Venezuela, the U.S. Dollar becomes King," The Washington Post, August 2, 2018. https://www.washingtonpost.com/world/in-socialist-venezuela-the-us-dollar-becomes-king/2018/08/01/7af16482-9442-11e8-818b-e9b7348cd87d_story.html?noredirect=on&utm_term=.be2ec2fc6695 (accessed January 1, 2019).
79 Julia Jones and Stefano Pozzebon, "Venezuela's Health System is in Worse Condition than Expected, Survey Finds," CNN, March 28, 2018. https://www.cnn.com/2018/03/28/americas/venezuela-hospitals-report/index.html (accessed November 23, 2018).

do not have basic utility services or food for school lunches.[80]

On a daily basis, Venezuelan bank managers establish new limits on the amount of money individual account holders may withdraw. These limits are based on the delivery of cash that banks receive from the Venezuelan Central Bank. That means each individual bank may have a different withdrawal limit on the same day; anywhere between 5,000-30,000 bolivars. As of Summer 2018, 10,000 bolivars equaled only .04 cents in USD. 300,000 bolivars equaled about $1.21 USD. In an effort to more easily transact business, the government dropped 5 zeros from this number and issued a new currency. Unfortunately, this move did not fix Venezuela's core problems; it only means that people will not have to carry as much cash in order to do business.

At present, many Venezuelan businesses will only accept USD for transactions. This excessively disadvantages the poor from making purchases while the rich pay dearly for goods and services if they don't have USD.[81] Even those who have jobs can no longer afford to purchase basic necessities such as food. Several government decisions contributed to the food shortage, including not growing food on government-owned farmland, choosing to pay off the country's debt instead of purchasing food for their citizens, and an increase in black market and other corrupt activities. In June 2018, a basic food basket consisting of rice, milk, beans, and other items cost 654,214,674 bolivars or $2,629 USD.[82] This is more than a basic Venezuelan wage

---

80 Editors, "Desercion Escolar Alcanza el 58% en Todo el Pais," Contexto Diario, July 17, 2018. http://contextodiario.com/venezuela/desercion-escolar-alcanza-el-58-en-todo-el-pais/ (accessed November 23, 2018).
81 Emiliana Disilvestro and David Howden, "Venezuela's Bizarre System of Exchange Rates," Mises Institute, January 7, 2016. https://mises.org/library/venezuelas-bizarre-system-exchange-rates (accessed November 23, 2018).
82 Editors, "Dictadura de Maduro Impide Marcha de Trabajadores de la Salud," Panam Post,

Historical Case Studies: Economic Collapse

of 27,091 bolivars plus the 63,720 government food bonus per month combined.[83] Hyperinflation in Venezuela thus currently means that those who are working do not earn enough in one month to purchase even one basket of food from the government. Consequently, a 2016 study found that 75% of Venezuelans have lost an average of 19 pounds due to this severe lack of food.[84]

Nearly 2.3 million people in a population of 32 Million have left Venezuela since 2014, primarily due to food shortages. Venezuelans have migrated to neighboring countries like Columbia, Ecuador, Peru, and Brazil.[85] Those who can afford it, and have passports, migrated even further away to places like Spain, Italy, and other countries.

Lack of food and other services have caused widespread protests and riots in the streets. Lootings and truck robberies in Venezuela are now commonplace.[86] These crimes are directly proportional to the increased number of hungry people. Bribery is the norm, and food as payment is preferred over the devalued currency. This signifies an evolving bartering system as Venezuela's currency is failing. In 2016, Venezuela had the second highest murder rate in the world (28,479). El Salvador

---

August 16, 2018. https://es.panampost.com/efe-panampost/2018/08/16/dictadura-maduro-salud/ (accessed November 23, 2018).
83 Editors, "Venezuela Minimum Wage Rate 2018," Minimum-Wage, December 2018. https://www.minimum-wage.org/international/venezuela (accessed November 23, 2018).
84 Andrew V. Pestano, "Venezuela: 75% of Population lost 19 Pounds amid Crisis," UPI, February 19, 2017. https://www.upi.com/Top_News/World-News/2017/02/19/Venezuela-75-of-population-lost-19-pounds-amid-crisis/2441487523377/ (accessed November 23, 2018).
85 EFE, "ONU, Preocupada Por el Exodo de Venezolanos, Pide Ayudar a Paises Vecinos," Panam Post, August 15, 2018. https://es.panampost.com/efe-panampost/2018/08/15/onu-exodo-venezolanos/ (accessed November 23, 2018).
86 Andrew Cawthorne, "Mad Max Violence Stalks Venezuela's Lawless Roads," Reuters, February 9, 2018. https://www.reuters.com/article/us-venezuela-economy-trucks-widerimage/mad-max-violence-stalks-venezuelas-lawless-roads-idUSKBN1FT1G9 (accessed November 23, 2018).

ranked number one.[87]

In 2015, President Obama issued Executive Order ("EO") 130808 which did not allow Venezuelan debts to last longer than 90 days, depending on the circumstances.[88] In a nutshell, no one is allowed to extend long-term credit or purchase long-term bonds from Venezuela. Some analysts believe the Venezuelan government was taking the funds and hoarding the money for their own personal gain, rather than using the money to feed the Venezuelan people or to improve the country's infrastructure. The unfortunate affect is that the government reduced their international purchases of food by about 30% in 2017 in order to meet $10 billion in debt payments, which was no longer extendable because of the executive order.

The trajectory of Venezuela's situation is an imminent failure in their currency, the collapse of their economy, and an increase in internal conflict which will result in more people dying by violence, lack of medical care, or starvation. Venezuelans relied heavily on their government to take care of them. As a result, the people were not prepared for what happened. Self-reliance came too little too late. Venezuelan citizens' increased reliance on the U.S. Dollar to survive in the short term may help to offset some of the effects of hyperinflation there. But in the longer term, when the U.S. dollar has its own currency crisis and hyperinflation follows in America, people in Venezuela and other countries around the world will have an even worse

---

87 Editors, "With 28,479 Killings, Venezuela takes Second Spot on World Murder Ranking," Elpais, December 29, 2016. https://elpais.com/elpais/2016/12/29/inenglish/1483016769_194171.html (accessed November 23, 2018).

88 Editors, "U.S. Economic and Trade Sanctions against Venezuela," Gibson Dunn, March 13, 2018. https://www.gibsondunn.com/wp-content/uploads/2018/03/WebcastSlides-US-Economic-and-Trade-Sanctions-Against-Venezuela-2018-03-13.pdf (accessed November 23, 2018).

situation to contend with if the underlying issues which caused the economic turmoil in those countries are not fixed.

Venezuela Update: Venezuela continues to experience hyperinflation. Prices increased again by more than 50% in October 2019 over September 2019.[89] Many have abandoned the bolivar and only use USD, the American currency. However, the government has put some restrictions on purchasing USD so many people use the black market.

When Venezuelans withdrawal money from the bank, they spend it immediately not knowing the currency worth later that day or how much the next day prices will increase. Many rely on relatives living abroad to send them money in order to survive.[90]

GERMANY: (1914-1924)

After World War I (also known as "The Great War"), Germany dethroned their Kaiser and became a democracy for a short period of time. This 'Weimar Republic' began in 1919 and lasted until 1933 when Adolf Hitler rose to power by proclaiming himself Führer of the new National Socialist German Worker's Party (or the Nazis).

In 1914, Germany funded World War I by abandoning the gold standard for their currency, and issuing war bonds to the German people.[91] At the time, they believed the war would only last a few months. Instead, it lasted for 4 years. Money was printed to pay for the war, municipality expenses, and loans for

---

89 Nihad Ahmed, "Venezuela Inflation September 2019", FocusEconomics, October 19, 2019, https://www.focus-economics.com/countries/venezuela/news/inflation/inflation-eases-to-seventh-month-low-in-september-amid-central, (accessed December 20, 2019).
90 Davis, Saliba, Morgan, "Venezuela: 1 litre of mild could cost a third of your wage|#TheCube", euronews, July 26, 2019, https://www.euronews.com/2019/02/15/venezuela-all-my-life-s-savings-were-destroyed-by-hyperinflation-thecube, (accessed December 20, 2019).
91 Adam Fergusson, When Money Dies (New York: William Kimber & Co. Ltd., 1975), p. 79.

industries. Shortly after the United States entered the Great War in 1917, Germany surrendered. The Treaty of Versailles imposed severe reparations on Germany to repay Allied war expenses. Prior to the war, the German Mark was valued at 20 to 1 against the Great British Pound (GBP) and 4.20 to 1 against the United States Dollar (USD). By the end of the war in November 1918, the mark was valued at 43 to 1 GBP and 5.11 to 1 USD.[92] By the time the Treaty of Versailles was signed in June 1919, the mark was 60 to 1 GBP.[93] And by December of 1919, the mark had hyper-inflated to 185 to 1 GBP.[94] But this was only the beginning.

Many factors contributed to Germany's hyperinflation after the Great War, including civil unrest, forced resignations and/or assassination of government leaders, the French invasion of the industrial region along the Ruhr River in Western Germany, as well as other economic and social issues. During all of this upheaval, the government continued to print money. And hyperinflation worsened. The effects on the German people were a devastating loss of wealth, homelessness, and death by starvation.

Prior to the war, an egg in Germany cost 4 pfennigs (about 4 cents).[95] By May 1922 that same egg had risen to 7.20 marks. By early 1923, the price of an egg had skyrocketed to 800 marks, and in May 1923, it cost 2,400 marks. Later that year, a liter (just over a quart) of milk increased from 1,800 to 3,800 marks, a kilo of flour (2.2 lbs.) went from 2,400 to 6,600 marks, and a kilo of pork went from 10,400 to 32,000 marks. Wages doubled during this time, but the price of goods had almost tripled.[96]

---

92 Frederick Taylor, The Downfall of Money (New York: Bloomsbury Press, 2013), p. 31.
93 Fergusson, When Money Dies, p. 16.
94 Ibid.
95 100 pfennigs equals 1 mark.
96 Fergusson, When Money Dies, p. 142.

Historical Case Studies: Economic Collapse

During this post-war inflation and subsequent hyperinflation, the middle and privileged classes lost most of their wealth and felt the effects even before the working class did. One reason is that the German government continued to subsidize the working class, especially those returning from war. As prices increased, the government increased wage and pension subsidies to keep up. These increases caused Germany's government to print more money.[97]

Many in the middle and privileged classes had professions with fixed salaries or lived off their investments. Thus, when prices for goods increased, they were unable to keep up with the cost of living. Much of their tangible wealth was sold or traded for food. Those who lived on fixed incomes not subsidized by the government, starved or froze to death from their inability to purchase food or coal to keep themselves warm in the winter months. Income that was meant to live on comfortably through retirement dried up fast as the cost of living spiraled out of control. In 1913, 15% of the wealth of German people was in investment income such as government bonds rather than earned wages. By 1923, that number fell to 3 percent.[98] Trying to stay ahead of price increases became a full-time occupation. As soon as workers got paid, they would immediately go to the market to purchase what they could, knowing that within hours, the prices would increase again.

Farmers who grew food and had livestock, those with gardens, and those who exchanged their marks for foreign currency including the USD, franc (FF), and GBP were able

---

97 Ibid., pp. 140-141, 143-144.
98 Holtfrerich, The German Inflation 1914-1923, p. 268.

to weather this hyperinflation turmoil. Those who exchanged their German marks to a foreign currency, and then changed back again the next day, made a fast profit because the price of the mark fell so quickly. The changing of marks to a foreign currency was done on a regular basis in order to try to stay ahead of the decreasing value of the mark. The government tried to stop this practice, but German citizens did not listen. Instead, they used the black market to exchange currencies.

Interestingly, those who had fixed-payment debts such as mortgages and rent fared well because the decreased currency value actually decreased their debt, making it easier to pay.[99] However, only a few were at an advantage in this way. Creditors, savers, and investors had significant declines in income.[100] The majority of Germans suffered financially during this time.

In about July 1922, the German economy hurtled into hyperinflation. Prices began rising by about 50% every month.[101] Because the mark depreciated so rapidly, the Reichsbank (Germany's Central Bank) started printing larger denominations of money from the 100,000 mark to the 1,000,000 mark and finally, 12 zeros were added. Prior to this, Germans had to carry sacks or large baskets to hold their currency. The *Manchester Guardian* reported the following story:

"There is a current story in Berlin of a woman who went shopping with a basket to carry her paper money. She put it down for a minute, and on looking around found that the basket had been stolen – but the paper money left behind!"

---

99 The German government put rent control into effect so that rents would not increase.
100 Taylor, The Downfall of Money, p. 206.
101 Ibid., p. 205.

Doctors, dentists, and other professionals demanded payment in food or another currency rather than the mark. Businesses that contracted work to be paid upon completion suffered because between the price quote and the work's completion, it often ended up costing more to produce a product than what they received in salary. This made it nearly impossible for businesses to keep up with pricing. As a result, many shut their doors.

One woman survived in 1923 at the height of Germany's hyperinflation put it this way:

"I offered her lard at 12 Billion to the pound, and she jumped at it. I found out afterwards that lard had gone up that afternoon from 12 to 16½ Billion. But I had bought a quantity of lard at 8 Billion some time ago. That is my latest 'device.' When I have marks that I want to dispose of quickly, I invest them in edibles of a durable nature. This is the most stable form of circulating medium. I can pay my library subscriptions in rice or dried plums, and my dentist's bill in condensed milk. Eggs, too, are greedily accepted. But for ordinary shopping this kind of specie has its drawbacks, even when you take the perambulator [measuring machine] with you as your purse."[102]

The drawback she is referring to is the inability to assess the actual price of a commodity upon purchase.

Finally, in November of 1923, Rentenbank, a new central bank, was created to replace the Reichsbank. Germany then created the Rentenmark currency. For a while both currencies circulated simultaneously. The valuation of the Rentenmark was set at 4.2 Trillion Mark to 1 USD and 18 Trillion Mark to 1 GBP. One Trillion paper marks equaled 1 Rentenmark,

---

102 Ibid., p. 320.

thus removing the 12 zeros.[103] War bond values were reduced from 154 Billion Marks to 15.4 pfennigs. Germany's post war debt was wiped out, and Germans who invested heavily in war bonds, lost everything. In effect, this was a currency reset.

THE CYPRUS EXPERIMENT

Cyprus is a Mediterranean island nation that belongs to the EU. Around 2012, several EU member nations faced financial problems, including Greece, Spain, Italy, and Cyprus. All of them turned to the EU for assistance. And the EU helped them all. Cyprus was unique, however, because it was used as a testing ground and was the only country where those who held accounts in Cyprus banks were required to help bail-out the banks in that country. This approach became known as the Bail-In Rescue Plan.[104]

As part of this plan, up to 37.5% of deposits were converted into Class A shares of stocks, while about 22.5% of deposits were temporarily frozen. Thus, someone with 100,000 euros in the Bank of Cyprus had 37,500 euros converted to stock and another 22,500 euros temporarily frozen leaving that person with an available balance of about 40,000 euros. In addition, the Bank of Cyprus limited daily withdrawals to about 300 euros. The effect on the depositors was a change in behavior due to lack of confidence in the banks. Deposits in Cyprus banks decreased as people held on to their cash. Even those who were not adversely affected by the bail-in withdrew money and increased their cash holdings as a result of this experiment.[105]

---

103 Ibid., pp. 328-329.
104 Editors, "Press Release by the Central Bank of Cyprus regarding the Resolution Measures Implemented at the Bank of Cyprus and Laiki Bank," Mondo Visione, March 30, 2013. http://www.mondovisione.com/media-and-resources/news/press-release-by-the-central-bank-of-cyprus-regarding-the-resolution-measures-im/ (accessed November 23, 2018).
105 Martin Brown, Ioanna Evangelou, and Helmut Stix, "Banking Crisis, Bail-ins and Money

Historical Case Studies: Economic Collapse

One key takeaway is that as a result of Cyprus' success in dealing with their financial crisis, the EU, Canada, and the United States <u>formalized</u> the Cyprus approach into laws requiring similar bail-in options in their own nations.[106] This means that what happened in Cyprus with individual accounts could happen in America as well. A significant factor to note regarding Cyprus is that the majority of their depositors were <u>not</u> Cyprus citizens. This may be why the tiny nation was chosen for the experiment. Protests were ongoing during this time of economic transition, but to my knowledge, no long lasting violence erupted.

Holdings," Central Bank of Cyprus Working Paper No. 2017-2, January 24, 2018. https://papers.ssrn.com/sol3/papers.cfm?abstract_id=3102815 (accessed January 1, 2019).
106 Phoenix Capita, "We've All Been Warned (the Cyprus "Bail-In" Model is Coming to a Country near You)," Zero Hedge, October 28, 2015. https://www.zerohedge.com/news/2015-10-28/weve-all-been-warned-cyprus-bail-model-coming-country-near-you (accessed January 25, 2019).

CHAPTER 7

The Coming Paradigm Shift for America

> *"What we see as valuable today will have no value during this time [of barter and trade]. And what we perceive as having no value today will have great value for trading while we are in this temporary system."*
>
> Word from the Lord, 2006

American culture contains a mixture of mindsets which include the capitalistic mindset as well as a socialistic mindset. The latter is evidenced in government social programs and the numerous non-profit organizations that service communities across the country. America's landscape is also open to people who have an entrepreneurial spirit – to carve out their own future. We have a system where, upon retirement, the older generation can receive benefits in the form of social security to assist with daily living and Medicare to aid in health care expenses. There are multiple food programs within the government sector and private sector that prevent anyone from starving. Although there is much room for improvement in multiple areas, there are systems in place that act as a net to catch those who have need of such services.

For many, these programs increase confidence in our government to take care of its population. But what if, even for a short period of time, the government was not able to pay for these programs? How would this effect Americans' confidence in their own government? If the decision were made to stop social welfare payments even for a month, the effect on public confidence would be severe due to the fact that peoples' ability to support themselves would be in jeopardy.

According to economist Martin Armstrong, the lack of the public's confidence in their government contributes to hyperinflation.[107] If the U.S. government was forced to honor derivative contracts and other debt generated by American banks, that could require them to suspend social services for a month or more. If this happens, Americans would begin to lose confidence in their government, especially given the government's mismanagement of the 2008 financial crisis.

But paying for default derivative contracts would not, by itself be enough to trigger a full loss of public confidence in my opinion. I believe instituting bail-ins (as happened in Cyprus) would begin to tip the scale closer to a confidence lag. If American taxpayers are forced to again pay for the banking industry's fiscal mismanagement, it would be seen as an erosion of individual civil liberties. As people's purchasing power for basic necessities begins to dwindle, confidence in the government would also decline. Suspending government services would further fuel this erosion of public confidence.

---

107 Martin Armstrong, "Here's How Hyperinflation Happens," GoldSilver, LLC, March 5, 2018, https://goldsilver.com/blog/martin-armstrong-heres-how-hyperinflation-happens/ (accessed February 7, 2019).

Another factor determining the American people's level of confidence in their government would be the confiscation of the individuals' assets. I am specifically speaking about gold. I would like to convey a scenario the Lord shared with me a few years ago. Since that time, much has shifted spiritually for America. What you are about to read is a possible outcome based on what happened with a previous executive order. I will describe what happened before and how it could possibly happen again.

WILL GOLD AND SILVER REALLY BE A SAFE HAVEN DURING THE NEXT ECONOMIC CRISIS?

Over the last few years I have been praying concerning the impending economic crisis, and I found it interesting that the Lord would say to me, "Silver, not gold." But I didn't understand why. Recently, the Lord deepened my understanding, and now I have an idea as to why, as an investment choice, silver will be safer than gold. But to lay the groundwork, we will have to travel back in time to 1917, 1933, and 1934.

During World War I, the Trading with the Enemy Act of 1917 was made into law. This act restricted trade with governments hostile to the United States during times of war. In 1933, the act was amended via the Emergency Banking Relief Act, expanding its scope to include national emergencies. But that's not all it did. The 1933 amendment also expanded presidential authority over **"export, hoarding, or earmarking of gold or silver coin."**[108] With this new law in place, President

---
108 Franklin D. Roosevelt, Public Papers of the President of the United States, 1933, Volume 2, "President Proclaims a Bank Holiday," (Washington, D.C.: The White House, 1938), p. 25. https://books.google.com/books?id=eibeAwAAQBAJ&pg=PA25&lpg=PA25&dq=%E2%80%9Cexport,+hoarding,+or+earmarking+of+gold+or+silver+coin.%E2%80%9D&source=bl&ots=acAI-YrQIT&sig=ACfU3U381OyYWtaYgAohUkbQ-MWxGphVUg&hl=en&sa=X&ved=2ahUKEwiN-LW3_a_gAhUCG6wKHbjwA-

Roosevelt signed Executive Order 6102 which <u>limited</u> the <u>ownership</u> of monetary gold by anyone, including a partnership, association, or corporation. This law required all American citizens to <u>turn their gold over</u> to the United States Treasury within 15 days of the notice. Not doing so could result in a fine of $10,000 or 10 years' imprisonment.[109] The only entities exempt from this new law were businesses that used gold in their products, such as dentists, jewelers, or artists. Everyone else had to comply. From this point forward, individual citizens were only allowed to own up to $100 worth of gold, but that was all.

EO 6102 has never expired; it's still on the books and can be re-activated, revised, or re-written into a similar but updated EO by any sitting U.S. president. Let's fast forward to the very near future and look at how this executive order with a modern president *could* unfold. If war breaks out or a national emergency is declared, an executive order like 6102 could be activated, triggering government confiscation of individually-owned precious metals.

Why would the government do this <u>again</u>? Such an order <u>might</u> slow down a hyperinflation event. Hyperinflation causes a country's currency to devalue at a very rapid pace. If that happened, all of our basic necessities would become very expensive, massive layoffs would ensue, and the government would have a hard time paying its bills, including benefit payments such as social security and Medicare. This would make it necessary to end the life of the U.S. Dollar. But before

---

YQ6AEwCXoECAcQAQ#v=onepage&q=%E2%80%9Cexport%2C%20hoarding%2C%20 or%20earmarking%20of%20gold%20or%20silver%20coin.%E2%80%9D&f=false (accessed February 9, 2019).

109 Tyler Durden, "What 40 Years of Gold Confiscation by the US Government Looks Like – Notice of Executive Order issued April 5, 1933," Zero Hedge, August 21, 2012. https://www.zerohedge.com/news/what-30-years-gold-confiscation-us-government-looks (accessed February 9, 2019).

the U.S. can initiate this currency reset, the treasury will need to prop up the country's value. This is the primary reason why the government would find it necessary to confiscate gold from We, the American People.

By way of reminder, another reason why America's value will need to be shored up is because other countries that have been trading in USD will begin to use other currencies which will facilitate the rapid decline in the value of the dollar. Currently, the purchase of oil around the world is traded in a currency known as petrodollars. In early 2018, China introduced crude oil futures contracts denominated in renminbi ("RMB"), the Chinese Yuan. The purpose was to promote China's currency for use in global trade.[110] Both Russia and China are pushing for options other than the USD in order to trade globally with their own currencies. If the dollar is removed as the main currency of the world economy, even in part, it will lead to excess USD circulating within the global market. Such a circumstance will intensify the inflation rate of the USD both within America and around the world.

The best and quickest way to shore up an asset is with gold. But short of the Federal Reserve printing more USD, and due to the surmounting U.S. deficit, the ability of the American government to purchase gold will be severely limited. So how will the United States obtain more gold? I believe that gold will be confiscated from the American people either via EO 6102 or a similar order.

What I am about to describe as a possible scenario is severe. When God gave me this scenario, it was based on

---

110 Grant Clark and Sungwoo Park, "China is About to Shake up the Oil Futures Market," Bloomberg, March 25, 2018. https://www.bloomberg.com/news/articles/2018-03-25/china-s-oil-futures-are-finally-here-what-you-need-to-know (accessed November 23, 2018).

a specific person holding the Office of the President. That person was Hillary Clinton. She did not win the election. It is not my intention to pull politics into the discussion, but in my opinion, the person elected to the presidency in 2020 will have a direct impact on what will happen with people's individual sovereignty, via whether and how the government confiscates individually-owned gold. The situation presented here is a worst case scenario. I present it to you in the hopes that we will not see it happen but we should prepare for it nonetheless.

Initially, the method the government uses to confiscate privately owned precious metals will be covert for two reasons: to avoid a panic and to keep a brave face on the situation. Americans will be asked, even enticed, to give up their gold through buyback programs possibly buying back gold at a perceived market value that is greater than gold's current value. Retirement accounts, pensions, and 401(k)s that have investments backed in gold, will receive extra cash in their accounts in exchange for the gold held in those accounts, put in place specifically to hedge off inflation.

The new executive order will look similar to EO 6102 but with some updates. I believe that our government will slowly become more overt in its efforts to confiscate gold from its citizens. Gold dealers will be required to turn over their customer lists to the Treasury, who in turn will use this information to force compliance with the new order. As mentioned previously, our government will initially try to look like the good guy. Owners of gold coin, bullion, and certificates will be offered a 'fair' price for their gold when they turn it in. The time period for the confiscation process will not be long. In 1933, it was 15 days. This time, it may be around the same time frame, or perhaps 30 days. Currently,

America is bankrupt and unable to pay its bills. But I believe the Treasury will print additional dollars in order to 'pay' for the gold.

The spin from the government will be that turning in your gold will be for the good of America, to help keep America's sovereignty and national security intact. I believe the population will be told that they will not lose any economic value since their gold will be exchanged for USD. After the initial time period to turn in gold has passed, agents from the Internal Revenue Service (IRS) will come into play. For example, if gold was purchased through any of the dealers who turned in their customer lists but you yourself did not turn in your gold by the deadline, you could be visited by an IRS agent who will already have the authority to search your home and seize assets via the new executive order. If this happens and they find gold after the allotted time, you would not be compensated. Instead, you would be fined and could face a prison sentence. If we happen to be at war as this EO is implemented, the very act of keeping your gold could be interpreted as treason. I realize that this scenario seems unlikely to happen in our country. But I mention it because it is a possibility and because of what the Lord has shown me. That being said, if something like this did happen, the only people to be negatively affected by it would be those who did not adhere to the executive order.

But this is not all that the American public will have to deal with. As a result of massive layoffs, lack of jobs, suspended social benefit payments, and increased panic among the American public, burglaries will also increase. For those who want to comply with the executive order, it may become very dangerous to do so. People will be in a lot of fear not knowing what to do. But the government will have little sympathy;

they will want the gold. Fear of robbery or even death will not be a defense against turning in gold during this time.

Usually, when the government acts aggressively within our borders, it's not published through the mainstream media. Our government is very careful of its image. But what's coming will be extraordinary. We will see the aggressiveness of the government's tactics played out before our eyes. They will tell us that what they are doing is for the good of our country and it's necessary in order for us to continue to be a sovereign nation.

After this short time period of gold confiscation, the United States will perform a currency reset on the U.S. Dollar, thereby wiping out our country's massive debt. <u>For those who received dollars for their gold trade-in, financial security will only be temporary. If the government announces that the dollar will be reset, its value will decrease once again</u>. For example, say a person turns in $10,000 worth of gold in exchange for the same value in dollars. **When the dollar resets, the exchanged value will be significantly less; about 50% to 60% less, maybe even more.** The $10,000 received will only be worth $4,000 to $5,000 after this reset. One way to minimize this disastrous outcome is a strategy the Lord showed me of establishing a currency kit. This will be discussed later in this book.

Silver coins may be part of the new executive order but the focus of the government is going to be on gold. Why? Because gold is what other nations around the world are currently purchasing and storing up. Since the EO confiscation period will be short, I believe that federal agents sent to seize it will focus on gold. But if they find silver in the process, they will keep it.

Gold is also expensive for many people, making it less accessible. Gold is finite. Although silver is less expensive than gold, it is also finite. Meaning there is only so much gold and silver, not everyone, even if they can afford it, will be able to get their hands on precious metals. I believe in the coming months and years prior to the collapse of the banks, gold and silver will become harder to find for purchase.

Many aspects of our lives will be harder in the not too distant future. The signs are already present in the marketplace. Next, we will take a look at some of the signs that our economic way of life is failing, as categorized by market sector. Know that what I will discuss is only a glimpse of the current state of affairs; a peak at what might be indicators of impending economic collapse, and a look at the possibility of what may happen in specific economic sectors.

CHAPTER 8

The First Wave – Rents

> *"Rents will increase rapidly. People will have to make a choice: to have money, to pay rent, or to purchase food. It will not be safe to obtain food from the government as it will require the mark (of the beast)."*
>
> Word from the Lord, August 2018

We are currently in the first wave of an economic downturn now; it started with the 2008 financial crisis. In the first wave, the economy will see a rise in the cost of living, in housing, and in food costs, as well as a squeeze on the middle class. The impact is gradual, so people go on with their lives. But in looking back 10 or 15 years, many will say that it has become harder over time to maintain the same standard of living.

The cost of housing including rents is skyrocketing across the nation. As a result, the homeless have a new face. No longer is it just those who are mentally ill or on drugs. Even those who hold steady jobs can easily find themselves homeless in our society. As of this writing, about 10% of the homeless population in San

Francisco, 8% in Los Angeles,[111] and 20% in Seattle all have jobs.[112] To give you an idea of the numbers, San Francisco has about 8,000 homeless, compared to Los Angeles County, which has more than 50,000 homeless. Seattle's last count in 2018 was just over 12,000 homeless. But I believe these numbers are low estimates. People who have no address are hard to keep track of and thus, to count. Also, many live with family or friends using their personal network to prevent them from having to live in their cars or on the streets. Besides those with a support system, only those who have the benefit of rent control or some other type of housing assistance fare better. The estimated number of homeless nationwide in 2018 was about 550,000.[113] That number is down from 647,000 in 2008. But as the economy worsens in the next few years, I believe the number of homeless will see a steep increase.

    I have a friend who at the time of this writing has four generations living in her home; children, grandchildren, great grandchildren, an ex-husband, and a cousin. I recently paid a visit and her house was crowded and busy. She wants to have her home to herself, but she allows her family to stay with her in order to help them. Other hindrances for families include laws that require them to rent a 3-bedroom apartment if there are 3 or more children. Generally, two bedrooms are less expensive than 3 bedrooms.

---

111 David Wagner, "Thousands of Californians are Working while Homeless, and Many Don't Want Their Boss to Know," *KQED*, August 22, 2018. https://www.kqed.org/news/11690325/thousands-of-californians-are-working-while-homeless-and-many-dont-want-their-boss-to-know (accessed November 23, 2018).

112 Monica Nickelsburg, "Homelessness and Jobs: What the Numbers Say," *Geekwire*, August 13, 2018. https://www.geekwire.com/2018/homelessness-employment-numbers-say-jobs-economy-housing-affordability/ (accessed November 23, 2018).

113 Editors, "US Homeless People Numbers Rise for First Time in Seven Years," *BBC*, December 6, 2017. https://www.bbc.com/news/world-us-canada-42248999 (accessed November 23, 2018).

Rents are creeping up, which is an indication of inflation. Even while the cost of purchasing a home has decreased somewhat, rents continue to increase. The United States median price for an unfurnished apartment in 2000 was $841. In 2008, the median price was $1,095. By 2017, it had climbed to $1,492.[114] This means that rents increased 23% between 2000 and 2008, and by another 27% between 2008 and 2017. The U.S. median price to purchase a home in 2000 was $119,600. By 2008, it had nearly doubled to $232,100. But by 2017, it had gone down to $199,200.[115] In 2008 and 2009, nationwide home prices fell due to the mortgage crisis. In the same time period, rents increased. As people moved away from home ownership due to foreclosure, the number of renters increased. Thirty-one percent of households rented in 2006. That number grew to almost 37% by 2016.[116] I believe landowners are attempting to squeeze the last bit of profit out of real estate ownership by way of increasing rents. Some of this rent increase can be contributed to cost pressures like increased in property values. City and county governments generate a large portion of their revenue from property taxes. Increased property values mean higher revenues for local governments. This cost is passed onto renters.

FOOD AND OTHER DAILY COMMODITIES

---

114 Editors, "Monthly Median Asking Rent for Unfurnished Apartments in the United States from 1980-2017," Statista, updated November 2018. https://www.statista.com/statistics/200223/median-apartment-rent-in-the-us-since-1980/ (accessed November 23, 2018).

115 Editors, "Historical Census of Housing Tables Home Values," U.S. Census Bureau, June 6, 2012. https://www.census.gov/hhes/www/housing/census/historic/values.html (accessed November 23, 2018).

116 Anthony Cilluffo, Abigail Geiger, and Richard Fry, "More U.S. Households are Renting Than at Any Point in 50 Years," Pew Research Center, July 19, 2017. http://www.pewresearch.org/fact-tank/2017/07/19/more-u-s-households-are-renting-than-at-any-point-in-50-years/ (accessed November 23, 2018).

Food and other items such as toiletries are also experiencing price increases. Recent tariff disagreements with other countries will put a strain on pricing for many of the items we are used to purchasing from overseas. This, in turn, will increase inflation. In 2018, it cost about $30.16 to purchase food for an individual compared to $20.00 in the year 2000. This represents a 50.79% increase in food prices over 18 years.[117] A typical consumer shopping basket consisting of various food staples plus gasoline was $72.64 in 2018. The price for these same items in 2008 was only $54.11.[118]

HEALTHCARE

Healthcare costs have increased by 43% since 2008. The Affordable Care Act (the "ACA" or "Obamacare") was passed in 2010 and was implemented in 2014. Health care costs started rising even before Obamacare took effect. For many Americans, the ACA did not make healthcare more affordable and did not increase plan and provider options. As a result, about 28.5 million people were without health insurance in 2017.[119]

AUTOMOBILE INDUSTRY

The automobile industry was also affected by the 2008 financial crisis. General Motors and Chrysler faced bankruptcy and requested $80.7 billion from the U.S. government to help bail them out. The next crisis will be worse for most sectors of our economy including the automobile industry. New car sales will shrink significantly because the middle class will no longer be

---

117 Editors, "Prices for Food: 2000-2018," U.S. Bureau of Labor Statistics, updated November 2018. http://www.in2013dollars.com/Food/price-inflation (accessed November 23, 2018).
118 Editors, "Our Price Basket," The People History, June 2018. http://www.thepeoplehistory.com/pricebasket.html (accessed November 23, 2018).
119 Edward R. Berchick, Emily Hood, and Jessica C. Barnett, "Health Insurance Coverage in the United States: 2017," U.S. Census Bureau, September 12, 2018. https://www.census.gov/library/publications/2018/demo/p60-264.html (accessed January 27, 2019).

able to afford them. Many cars will be repossessed, so there will be a large inventory of used cars. Those who are still able to pay their car notes may fare well because as inflation increases, car notes actually become cheaper. However, the strain will cause layoffs. Thus, support services like automobile insurance providers will also diminish.

GLOBAL CONFLICTS

I don't know specifics, but in the first wave, there will be an increase in global conflicts. As I was praying, the Lord showed me that in early 2019, something significant will happen in the Middle East to fuel the beginning of what may turn out to be World War III.

Our world economy is intricately intertwined on many levels including financially, even with those who are perceived as, shall we say, not so friendly. If we <u>do</u> enter into another global war, I believe the conflict will start with attacks on national economies in order to weaken countries that have global influence like the United States, China, and Russia. These attacks, will affect our financial structures like our banking and credit systems, and economic interactions, like the ability to purchase consumer goods. The purpose will be to weaken and prime the structures for a complete collapse. These types of attacks will happen in the second wave.

The first wave will continue to escalate through 2021 or 2022. During this time, inflation will continue to increase, its pace becoming more rapid until we hit hyperinflation. We will probably see hyperinflation begin sometime in 2021 or possibly a little sooner. This estimate is based on what the Lord showed me relating to the timing of the banking collapse.

There are action steps that can be taken during this period

of escalating inflation to help the reader financially survive the second wave. It's not too late, and anyone can take these steps; not just those who can afford to purchase gold, but anyone who has ears to hear can prepare for what is coming. You may even come out on the other side in a better financial position.

Prophetic Update: I believe the significant actions in the Middle East that could be a seed for World War III is the increased tensions between the United States and Iran. The tension began as a result of the United States withdrawal from the JCPOA or Joint Comprehensive Plan of Action otherwise known as the Iran Nuclear deal in May, 2018 between China, France, Germany, Russia, the United Kingdom and the United Stated States.

In April 2019, the Trump Administration formally designated Iran's Islamic Revolutionary Guard Corps (IRGC) as a Foreign Terrorist Organization (FTO) under section 219 of the Immigration and Nationality Act.

In May 2019, the United States increased their presence in the Middle East. In response, Iran threatened to not hold up their end of the JCPOA deal. Although the U.S. is no longer part of the deal, some European nations have also backed off in large part because of the strong influence the U.S. has on them, including the threat of increasing tariffs on European goods.

In June 2019, Iran shot down a U.S. drone claiming it breached Iranian land. Also, in June, two tankers were attacked which had been blamed on Iran. Iran admits to shooting down the drone but denies attacking the oil tankers.

As of the writing of this update, tension continues to increase near the Strait of Hormuz, a small canal where oil tankers pass near the Iranian border. Thirty percent of the world's oil passes through the canal. The U.S. has also increased their military presence in the area. Part of the reason why there is a looming threat for war is because since the U.S. pulled out of the agreement, in part as a result of the intelligence that came out of Israel, countries are forced to take sides regarding who to trade oil with and the currency used to trade.

In January 2020, the U.S. killed Qasem Soleimani, a Major General of the IRGC. In retaliation, Iran struck U.S. targets in Iraq. Waring words are traded between the two countries and tensions have increased significantly in the region.

In my opinion, Iran is not militarily powerful enough to take on the United States without other major sovereign powers on their side. What would be necessary for a third World War would be the agreement of major military players like China and Russia. But before there will be a military conflict of this magnitude, I believe we will see attacks in the areas of cyber and economics.

CHAPTER 9

The Second Wave – Hyperinflation

> "Hyperinflation can take virtually your entire life's savings, without the government having to bother raising the official tax rate at all."
>
> Thomas Sowell[120]

The second wave of the coming financial crisis will start towards the end of 2020 or the beginning of 2021. Hyperinflation will begin during this time. Recall that hyperinflation is when prices increase by at least 50% in one month.[121] Thus far, we have seen about a 32% increase in the cost of living since 2008. It hurts, but we live with it. As time passes, prices will continue to rise, but at a much faster rate. By the standard of the 2018 consumer shopping basket priced at $72.64, hyperinflation would mean paying $72.64 one month for the same items that you'll pay $108.96 for the next month. Even if hyperinflation drops back down to 30% a month later, this would mean the shopping basket could still cost the consumer $141.65 by the third month; twice the amount of 2018 prices.

Layoffs will increase during this time. More people will apply

---

120 Thomas Sowell, "Inflation is the Most Insidious Invisible Tax," Standard Times, December 14, 2012. http://archive.gosanangelo.com/opinion/thomas-sowell-inflation-is-the-most-insidious-invisible-tax-ep-438907590-355868741.html (accessed January 27, 2019).
121 Hanke and Krus, "World Inflations," 10.

for government assistance, putting a strain on federal resources. But government help will be slow to keep up with rising prices. The homeless population will increase among the unemployed because people will not be able to afford rents or a mortgage. As in 2008, this second wave will see an increase in foreclosures, and car repossessions. Crimes such as burglaries will also increase as people become desperate. I believe there will also be an increase in break-ins where food is kept, such as groceries stores and restaurants.

Unofficial markets sometimes referred to as the Black Market, will continue to grow in the U.S. These markets exist today, but they will become more visible and accessible as people become desperate to obtain needed goods after retail prices start to skyrocket. The reader may not be aware, but in many communities around the country, usually in urban areas, Black Market goods can be found at less than retail prices. Generally these goods have been stolen. As demand for these products at affordable prices increases across multiple economic and racial groups, I believe theft will increase as well. Additionally, people will increasingly sell personal items at auctions and pawn shops in order to pay for food. Times will be desperate for many more people than the number who were affected in 2008. Lootings and riots will increase. To maintain a calm citizenry, the government will increase social assistance to provide food and possibly even housing.

THRIFT STORES AND DISCOUNT STORES

The number of thrift and second hand stores nationwide has surpassed 25,000 and their rate of growth is about 7% per year.[122] Dollar stores also have over 25,000 locations nationwide.

---

122 Editors, "Industry Statistics & Trends," Narts, updated January 2015. https://www.narts.org/i4a/pages/index.cfm?pageid=3285 (accessed November 23, 2018).

The Second Wave – Hyperinflation

But many of these store's products are imported from China or other Pacific Rim countries. It is possible that these stores will not survive due to pricing pressures resulting from tariff wars. In the short term, however, as retail prices continue to rise, more people will flock to these discount stores for their goods. But even the discount stores will eventually have to raise their prices, too.

INTEREST RATES

Currently, the Federal Reserve is decreasing interest rates in order to stimulate the economy. Going into the second wave, interest rates will most likely increase. We will begin to see negative interest rates on bank accounts. This is sometimes disguised as early withdrawal fees or a monthly maintenance fee.

PETRODOLLAR

The Petrodollar is currency received from the sale of oil. The USD is the dominant global reserve currency and has been since 1944. Even oil uses USD as its trading currency. The term 'petrodollar' was created during the oil shortages of the 1970s.[123] Yet, the USD remained the global trading currency even when it went off the gold standard.

China currently purchases some of its oil using the petro-yuan. In the spring of 2018, China began trading oil hedges at about 2%.[124] By the fall, that amount had risen to almost 12%. And there are indications that Russia wants to follow suit.[125] This is important because as the USD is pushed out as the dominant world reserve

---

123 James Chen, "Petrodollars," Investopedia, updated November 20, 2017. https://www.investopedia.com/terms/p/petrodollars.asp (accessed November 23, 2018).
124 Oil hedges are the process of locking in a future selling price.
125 Georgi Gotev, "Russia Ditches Dollar, Opts for Euro and Yuan," Euractiv, January 11, 2019. https://www.euractiv.com/section/economy-jobs/news/russia-ditches-dollar-opts-for-euro-and-yuan/ (accessed February 16, 2019).

currency, more dollars will be in circulation putting pressure on the value of the dollar. Excessive dollars will flow back into the U.S. increasing the money supply and fueling inflation. To decrease the negative effects of this dominant currency shift, I believe the Federal Reserve will increase interest rates at an accelerated pace. However, I don't believe the measure will be effective.

MARTIAL LAW

Well into the second phase of the coming economic crisis, I believe Martial Law will be implemented in certain parts of the United States. Below is a comprehensive explanation of how this system could affect ordinary citizens:

"Martial Law is a system of absolute military control over all military and civilian activities of a country, in a theoretical or actual war zone, during civil disorder, in occupied territory, after a coup d'état, or during a state of emergency caused by a natural disaster such as an earthquake or a flood. In the United States only the President as Commander-in-Chief has authority to impose Martial Law and it must be limited to the duration of the warfare or emergency. It cannot be imposed in a manner resulting in a long-term denial of constitutional rights."

"Martial Law seeks to maintain public order in times of crisis, when the normal institutions of justice either cannot function or could be deemed too slow or too ill-equipped for the new situation. Usually Martial Law reduces some of the personal rights ordinarily granted to the citizen, limits the length of the trial process, and prescribes more severe penalties than ordinary law."[126]

---

126 Editors, "Legal Definition: Martial Law," US Legal, January 2016. https://definitions.uslegal.com/m/martial-law/ (accessed February 3, 2019).

The Second Wave – Hyperinflation

In some cities, this will only be a temporary measure to ensure domestic tranquility, but in other places, the military may need to stay longer. Although I don't know the catalyst for the imposition of Martial Law, civil unrest will increase across many metropolitan cities. The military will also be deployed overseas as tensions in the Middle East increase. If we are to have one, I believe the Middle East will be the birthplace of World War III.

EXODUS

Living in America will become more difficult as prices increase and people fear for their safety in public due to increased civil unrest, robberies, and murders. An exodus out of cities and into the suburbs and rural America will occur as people seek social stability and safety. This resettlement phenomenon is not new. America saw two previous 'Great Migrations' of those in dire financial straits. Between 1910 and 1970, six million decedents of slaves moved from the American South to the North, Northeast, West, and Midwest seeking better opportunities.[127] Likewise, the Dust Bowl which brought severe winds and drought to Oklahoma, Texas, New Mexico, Colorado, and Kansas between 1930 and 1940 caused the second Great Migration in America. This weather phenomenon propelled 3.5 million people westward, primarily into California, again, seeking a better life.[128]

WHAT WILL HAPPEN TO MY MONEY?

As the economy worsens, the strain on banks will increase across the globe. At some point during the second wave of

---
[127] Editors, "The Great Migration, 1910-1970," U.S. Census Bureau, September 13, 2002. https://www.census.gov/dataviz/visualizations/020/ (accessed November 23, 2018).
[128] Donald Worster, Dust Bowl: The Southern Plains in the 1930s (Oxford: Oxford University Press, 2004), p. 49. https://www.amazon.com/Dust-Bowl-Southern-Plains-1930s/dp/0195174887 (accessed January 29, 2019).

the economic crisis, the banks will finally collapse ... silently. I believe the first indicator of imminent banks failures will be their suspension of ATM withdrawals and temporary closures of brick and mortar banks. I don't think the general public will immediately be aware that there is anything wrong with access to their own money. I think we will be told that there is an electronic malfunction of some sort and it will be 'fixed' in a day or two. However, this "malfunction" will probably occur at all American banks, within the same general timeframe. For at least a few days, things will go on as normal. People will borrow cash from family and friends to tide them over until the banks reopen, thinking things will normalize in a few days. But days will turn into a week, possibly even a few weeks, with either no access or only limited access to personal accounts. Then there will be a total collapse of America's banking and financial system. No one knows specifically what a total collapse will look like but it will likely mean that we will have limited or no ability be able to use our debit or credit cards to make purchases. We will also likely be limited in our daily withdrawal of cash. Although my focus is on the United States, this collapse will be worldwide. Eventually, the banks will operate normally, but not before a lot of financial damage is realized in peoples' lives.

THE ARROGANCE OF THE DOLLAR

Hyperinflation will also take its toll on the American public. But I don't think the Federal Reserve is going to print larger denominated bills as we have seen happen in other nations. Since many of our transactions are electronic, printing larger bills will not be necessary. The Federal Reserve will continue to think they have control over the monetary system in our country. But we may be so indebted to other nations, that the Federal Reserve may be dismantled in favor of another financial system. Many in leadership positions will strongly believe that the dollar will regain its value. In that way, stubbornness will set in. In other words, the government may not make necessary economic policy adjustments in a timely manner so as to correct bank failures and thereby, save Americans from the financial destitution that leads to poverty and homelessness. Our federal government's actions may be the final straw in obliterating the American people's confidence in our elected officials. When trust fails in governments, people tend to hoard money and not invest it. Russia has started to divest from America.[129] In December 2017, Russia owned $102.2 billion in U.S. Treasury bonds. By May of 2018, that amount had plummeted to $14.9 billion.[130] That $87.3 billion drop represents an 85% decrease in Russia's investment in U.S. bonds. And that divestment occurred in less than six months' time. This very well could be a sign that lack of confidence in America's financial system has already begun.

Update: As of the third quarter, 2019, Russia's investment in Treasury bonds is $10 billion. A drop of an additional $4.9 billion.[131]

---

129 South Front, "Russian Share in the U.S. Debt is Getting Close to Zero," Robin Westen, RA, October 18, 2018. http://robinwestenra.blogspot.com/2018/10/russia-is-divesting-itself-of-american.html (accessed January 27, 2019).
130 Matt Egan, "Russia dumped 84% of its American debt. What that Means," CNN Business, July 30, 2018. https://money.cnn.com/2018/07/30/investing/russia-us-debt-treasury/index.html (accessed February 9, 2019).
131 Sputnik News, "Russia continues to Dump US Treasury Bonds", SGT Report, August 16, 2019, https://www.sgtreport.com/2019/08/russia-continues-to-dump-us-treasury-bonds/, (accessed December 27, 2019).

CHAPTER 10

Preparation for Dark Days Ahead

> *"Your currency will be no more. What wealth will you have without the dollar? You must plan now. Sit with Me and I will give you specific instructions."*
>
> Word from the Lord, October 2006

THE LORD GIVES US TIME TO PREPARE

In the fall of 2006, God showed me what is coming to America. Shortly after that initial vision, I began praying for a covering or safety net. I remembered that in God's Word, He protected the righteous from His judgment, when it was close at hand.

In Genesis 6-7, God instructed Noah to build an ark which would ultimately save him, his family, and the earth's animals from destruction. In Genesis 19, God delivered Lot and his family from His judgment of Sodom and Gomorrah. God didn't begin destroying these cities until Lot and his family members were safe. In Genesis 41, God gave Joseph the interpretation of Pharaoh's dream: there would be 7 years of plenty and 7 years of famine. With God's wisdom, Joseph helped Egypt prepare during the years of plenty in order to survive during the years of famine that were to come. Thus, Egypt, their people, and peoples from other nations were saved from starvation.

A financial famine is coming to the United States of America that will spread like a wild fire. As a result, many people will become homeless and hungry. Right now, God is giving us a window of time to prepare for what is coming. About eight years ago, the Lord showed me some strategies for His people. One of the strategies He revealed was a currency kit to be discussed later in this book. This currency kit will function as both a safety net and a mechanism to facilitate wealth transfer. For those who harken and prepare, there will be a great wealth transfer. God encourages this type of preparation in His Word:

> *"A good man leaves an inheritance to his children's children, but the wealth of the sinner is stored up for the righteous."*
>
> Proverbs 13:22 (NKJV)

> *"But thou shalt remember the LORD thy God: for it is He that giveth thee power to get wealth, that He may establish His covenant which He sware unto thy fathers, as it is this day."*
>
> Deuteronomy 8:18 (KJV)

> *"For God gives wisdom and knowledge and joy to a man who is good in His sight; but to the sinner He gives the work of gathering and collecting, that he may give to him who is good before God."*
>
> Ecclesiastes 2:26 (NKJV)

Church, we are the ones who please God. We are His righteous and there is going to be a great wealth transfer after the U.S. dollar collapses. Our Father in Heaven wants us to prepare now, so that we can be His hands and feet in the earth during the coming financial crisis. Those who have ears to hear will be sustained, have the ability to help others, and further God's Kingdom upon the earth.

STRATEGIC ECONOMIC PREPAREDNESS

Many of us have heard or read economists' predictions about stock market crashes, recessions, and other economic doom and gloom scenarios. Even those who listen to prophetic messages from various ministries have heard similar information. It seems we are bombarded with information about what is coming to America. What should we do with this information? How do we prepare? Where do we begin? The Internet is filled with videos about preparing for catastrophe. Ready.gov, an official site of the Department of Homeland Security, is one of many websites that publishes information about preparing for the worst.[132] But how do we financially prepare? What should we do with our 401(k) plans, money market accounts, and other tangible and liquid assets?

What I share here should be considered financial

---
132 Editors, "Plan Ahead for Disasters," Ready.gov. https://www.ready.gov/ (accessed November 23, 2018).

suggestions, or allegorical examples of how to prepare based on individual situations. I have received some of these strategies through prayer. Others are common sense and practical advice. There are so many variables when it comes to individual and family financial situations that no one path will work for or fit everyone's life. What one person decides to do should not be construed as a better path than a different approach that someone else chooses. Everyone must consider his/her own situation and ask God for wisdom regarding the best path to take.

CHAPTER 11

Wealth will Not Disappear; It will be Transferred

> *"The wealth transfer that will take place during this decade is the greatest wealth transfer in history. ...Wealth is never destroyed it is merely transferred. And that means that on the opposite side of every crisis, there is an opportunity."*
>
> Mike Mahoney[133]

I believe the information and strategies in this book will provide an avenue for wealth transfer. An American and/or worldwide economic collapse does not mean that everyone will become poor or financially destitute. In fact, during economic downturns, wealth does not disappear; it is transferred from one party to another. Some say that the rich keep getting richer. Yet, the additional wealth that the rich

---
[133] Mike Mahoney, "Hidden Secrets of Money, Episode 2: Seven Stages of Empire," YouTube, August 13, 2013. https://www.youtube.com/watch?v=EdSq5H7awi8 (accessed February 9, 2019).

accumulate does not grow on trees in their backyards. Wealth comes from someone else trading out their holdings. Positioning yourself financially <u>before</u> the next economic downturn has the potential to transfer wealth <u>to</u> you. I believe God wants to transfer wealth to those who understand that such wealth is not solely for material possessions like cars, houses, clothes, etc. The coming wealth transfer will be for God's Kingdom purposes, to meet the Body of Christ's physical needs, and act as a light in the darkness.

> *"Nothing is better for a man than that he should eat and drink, and that his soul should enjoy good in his labor. This also, I saw, was from the hand of God. For who can eat, or who can have enjoyment, more than I? For God gives wisdom and knowledge and joy to a man who is <u>good</u> in His sight; but to the sinner He gives the work of gathering and collecting, that he may give to him who is good before God."*
>
> Ecclesiastes 2:24-26 (NKJV)

Now that you have the information necessary to begin preparations for coming economic collapse, keep reading to learn one of the strategies you can use to position yourself for a wealth transfer.

CHAPTER
12

The Bridge Currency Kit™

> *"Eye has not seen, nor ear heard, nor have entered into the heart of man the things which God has prepared for those who love Him."*
>
> 1 Corinthians 2:9 (NKJV)

The Bridge Currency Kit™ is a tool or system for purchasing and holding specific foreign currencies for the purpose of trading and bartering during the impending economic collapse. It is also a potential means for wealth transfer as the financial balance of power in the world shifts in the wake of this financial and economic crisis.

The Bridge Currency Kit™ contains specific currencies from countries that have strong holdings in gold, as well as large amounts of industrial and natural resources. Those who understand the times we are in generally advise that people purchase and hold gold and silver. However, the strategy that the Lord shared with me is to purchase and hold the currencies from countries that are doing just that … purchasing and storing gold and silver. I believe purchasing the fiat currency from these nations will add a layer of security because foreign currencies will be less likely confiscated by the U.S. government in the event that EO 6102 or something similar is once again implemented. Thus, it will be financially safer to hold these currencies than gold or silver.

The U.S. Dollar is valued against other currencies around the world. When the USD is strong, we get more for it in other countries. When our dollar is weak, we get less. In a worst case scenario, if the USD loses much of its value in an economic collapse, some of the world's other currencies will be worth a lot more. However, not all other currencies will experience this value increase. Thus, selecting the right currencies to hold as a hedge against a devalued U.S. Dollar will require wisdom, discernment, and prayer.

In addition, if banks fail and close their doors, obtaining certain world currencies may be restricted or prevented for political reasons. Exchanging USD for foreign currencies now, when those currencies are less expensive, will most likely net an increase in value later. In other words, when the USD decreases in value, I believe these specific currencies will increase in value.

Another very important reason to have a Bridge Currency Kit™ is because anyone, regardless of their economic situation, can purchase foreign currency. It is an exchange of one form of currency for another. This can be done in nominal denominations. When I check for news concerning the economy and how to protect oneself the advice I read or hear over and over again is to purchase gold in order to protect your assets. Some recommend buying both gold and silver, but more often,

The Bridge Currency Kit™

gold is the asset advocated by mainstream brokers of precious metals. The problem I have with this suggestion is that not everyone who belongs to God has the ability to purchase gold. Currently, gold costs $1,480 per ounce. While it is true that gold coins can be purchased at a fraction of an ounce reducing the price, even a fourth of an ounce is out of reach for many people.

In addition, if gold becomes at risk of confiscation by the federal government, then your Bridge Currency Kit™ will be safe. Trading dollars for the currencies in the kit will be less noticed by the federal government than purchasing gold at an authorized dealer. The Bridge Currency Kit™ will fly under the radar mainly because no one that I am aware of has suggested this strategy.

While praying over a few years' time, God revealed to me the currencies that should be part of The Bridge Currency Kit™. Consider this a short list. There may be other currencies that will thrive during the next global economic crisis as well, but I have confidence in the ones listed below. God told me that the far-eastern nations will fare better during the coming economic crisis, which is why there is a high mix from those countries below. Although I have every confidence in the list provided in this book, the reader is reminded to <u>pray</u> and consider their own unique situation before making any purchasing decisions.

- **Chinese Yuan / Renminbi ("CNY" or "RMB")**
- **Indian Rupee ("INR")**
- **Brazilian Real ("BRL")**
- **New Zealand Dollar ("NZD")**
- **United Arab Emirates' Dirhams ("AED")**

- **Indonesian Rupiah ("IDR")**

China – As of this writing, China has the largest economy in the world. The second largest is the European Union, and third is the United States.[134] China currently holds at least 15,000 tons of gold.[135] In addition, China is inserting their CNY into the oil and futures markets hoping to replace the petrodollar in global markets. China has great influence over other large Asian nations who trade on the world stage. At some point, nations will be forced to secure alliances. If there is a World War III, it is not clear how the war will play out and who will align with whom.

India – India and China are the biggest consumers of gold in the world. Gold is an integral part of Indian culture. Gold jewelry is often used for gifts at weddings and other ceremonies. This precious metal is also offered to Hindu gods. Deities have rights in India, so such gold offerings cannot easily be confiscated by the government.[136] Gold is also a savings vehicle for many people. Indian citizens prefer to hold their wealth in gold rather than in the banking system. Only one third of India's population has savings accounts.[137] The nation has a lot of gold, but its citizens, not the government, retain control of it.

India's possession of a significant amount of gold places her in a very good position if the world economic system, in whole or in part, returns to a gold standard. If India's government

---

134 Kimberly Amadeo, "China's Economy and Its Effect on the U.S. Economy," The Balance, November 23, 2018. https://www.thebalance.com/china-economy-facts-effect-on-us-economy-3306345 (accessed November 23, 2018).
135 Silver Fortune, "How Much Gold Does China Really Have?" The Daily Coin, June 30, 2018. https://thedailycoin.org/2018/07/01/how-much-gold-does-china-really-have-with-louis-cammarosano-video/ (accessed November 23, 2018).
136 David Chapman, "A Love Affair: India and Gold," BMG Group, March 23, 2016. http://bmg-group.com/love-affair-india-gold/ (accessed November 23, 2018).
137 Ibid.

adopted a gold standard for the INR, citizens may decide to gradually exchange their gold for the currency. Since 2016, there has been an increase in electronic purchases of gold via smart phones and e-wallets.[138] Moving away from physical currency and trading currency electronically may be the mechanism that will move gold from the hands of the citizens to the government, thus strengthening the INR on a global scale.

Brazil – While writing *The Bridge*, God showed me that the United States and Canada are going to do more business with Brazil in the future. In addition, Brazil will become a dominant nation in international trade. Brazil is the fifth largest country in the world, but is, in many ways, still a third world nation. I believe God has shown me that their status will change. Looking for proof in the natural, I ran across the promise of their new president elect Jair Bolsonaro to privatize state-owned companies, open up the economy through new trade agreements, and lower import tariffs. These policies will strengthen Brazil's international trade, thus transforming Brazil into a leading financial world player. Also, if there were to be another global war, I believe Brazil will remain neutral in the conflict, focusing instead on manufacturing and trade. This is similar to U.S. foreign policy at the beginning of World Wars I and II. Such neutrality will strengthen both Brazil's economy and currency, the BRL.

New Zealand – New Zealand has a strong open economy and several gold mines. If the world's nations shift the standard of their currencies either to gold or other natural assets, then New Zealand will be in a very good financial position. The NZD is

---

138 Editors, "In India, More People are Buying and Selling Gold Electronically," Learning English, April 1, 2018. https://learningenglish.voanews.com/a/in-india-more-people-buying-and-selling-gold-electronically/4313396.html (accessed November 23, 2018).

valued against the USD. When the USD goes into hyperinflation, the NZD will also suffer. My guess is that before hyperinflation sets in, New Zealand will switch their currency to a gold standard and/or a basket of currencies rather than the USD. By doing so, New Zealand will more easily weather the global economic downturn.

United Arab Emirates ("UAE") – Currently, the financial capital of the world is the London financial district also known as the City of London located in London, England. Last year, it was New York City, New York. Dubai, in the UAE is currently ranked 18th.[139] However, I believe that the coming economic downturn will significantly impact the United States and Europe by devaluing both the USD and the Euro. This, in turn, will cause the financial centers in both New York and London to crash. However, I also believe that London will rally; regaining some financial footing in her recovery period after the crash. But, I don't believe she will ever again be the world's financial center.

Regarding New York's financial center – I get a vision of a wasteland; almost like a war zone after a battle. I don't know the catalyst for what I am seeing, but actual buildings were leveled to the ground, similar to the aftermath of 9/11/2001. The difference between 9/11 and the vision I've seen is that this future devastation will physically affect many, many more people and buildings.

With these leading centers of finance reduced to rubble, I believe Dubai, UAE will become the world's financial center. Currently, the UAE's economy is strong and growing. I believe many of her assets will be shielded from the coming economic crisis. Dubai

---

139 Ben Moshinsky, "The 20 Most Powerful Financial Centres in the World," Business Insider, September 12, 2017. https://www.businessinsider.com/most-powerful-financial-centres-gfci-index-for-2017-2017-9?r=UK (accessed January 28, 2019).

has a vibrant and active precious metals market called the Dubai Gold Souk. A souk is a traditional marketplace located in the heart of Dubai's commercial district, Deira. For this reason, it's likely that the UAE also has enough precious metals stashed away to sustain themselves during the coming economic crisis.

Indonesia – Indonesia is emerging in the Asian financial and economic markets. Indonesia is also one of the top 10 gold mining countries in the world.[140] Their current gold reserves stand at 78.50 tons.[141] I don't know the specifics as to why the Lord told me to add Indonesia's currency to The Bridge Currency Kit™, but Indonesia possesses gold and has the ability to increase their holdings through mining. In the future, when gold holdings for countries become important as economies become partially tied to gold, Indonesia will be poised to benefit on the world economic stage. I also believe Indonesia's industry will increase around the globe, moving them to a more visible platform worldwide.

---

140 Editors, "Gold," Indonesia Investments, October 13, 2015. https://www.indonesia-investments.com/business/commodities/gold/item167 (accessed January 28, 2019).

141 Editors, "Gold Reserves: Asia," Trading Economics, updated January 2019. https://tradingeconomics.com/country-list/gold-reserves?continent=asia (accessed January 28, 2019).

CHAPTER 13

How to Exchange Currency

> *"Money is the opposite of the weather. Nobody talks about it, but everybody does something about it."*
>
> Rebecca Johnson[142]

Currencies can be purchased at national banks, currency exchange centers, or online. When changing currency, expect to pay an exchange fee. This fee will vary depending on the currency and the medium you use to purchase currency. For example, an exchange center at the airport charges higher rates than do online vendors or banks. In addition to exchange fees, some vendors require a minimum purchase amount. As of this writing, Wells Fargo required a $200 minimum purchase on their website. Note that

---

142 Rebecca Johnson, "Nobody Talks of Money," Made of Money, July 8, 2018. https://itsamoneything.com/money/rebecca-johnson-nobody-talks-of-money/#.XGjjUrhMFPY (accessed February 16, 2019).

if you purchase online, you will also be charged for shipping.

For reference purposes only, I have listed a few websites[143] that sell world currencies online:

1. Travelex – https://www.travelex.com/

2. International Currency Express, Inc. – http://foreignmoney.com/

Major banks[144] also offer world currency purchases online. Below are two examples:

1. Wells Fargo – https://www.wellsfargo.com/foreign-exchange/index

2. Bank of America – https://www.bankofamerica.com/foreign-exchange/foreign-currency-exchange.go

If you decide to purchase currency at a bank, then larger banks like Wells Fargo or Bank of America are probably a better option than smaller local banks. Smaller banks do not typically offer currency exchange as a service. Be aware that tellers have been trained to ask prying questions. I have yet to enter a bank that did <u>not</u> inquire if I was taking a trip or why I wanted the currency. Be careful! Although you are not doing anything wrong, it is wise to be vague with your answers. It's none of anyone else's business why you are exchanging currency. You can also spread your currency purchases across multiple banks, and/or purchase currency online. If you are planning to exchange large amounts of money, you don't want too many people knowing your business since you will be physically

---

[143] A company's placement on this list is for informational purposes only, and does not represent the author's specific endorsement of any goods or services offered by these websites.

[144] Again, the author does not endorse the goods or services offered by these specific banks.

storing these currencies. You could tell prying bank tellers that you intend to take a trip. If the bank does not have currency on hand, they can order it for you. Generally, banks will keep currencies on hand that are in the most demand such as the Euro.

I would not recommend keeping currency or even gold and silver in a safe deposit box at a bank. Safe deposit boxes are owned by the banks; customers rent them. When banks become insolvent during times of economic crisis, the FDIC can potentially confiscate the contents of safe deposit boxes.

Keeping currency, like gold and silver with you where you live is a better option because you will have quick access to these assets. That being said, when people get desperate and they know you have valuables in any form, you are vulnerable to break-ins. So, use caution and pray for discernment. Friends and family talk. You don't want to set yourself up for robbery. Discretion is important!

HIDE IN PLAIN SIGHT

Be prayerful about asset storage. Some people use multiple locations in their homes. Foreign currency, gold, and silver are also an inheritance. You may choose to store these assets in multiple places for security purposes. Then, in case something happens to you, consider telling only those you implicitly trust about these locations. You might consider telling only one person about a specific location and another person about a different location as a safety precaution. In this way, not everyone will know all the locations in which you store assets, thus safeguarding your wealth.

Again, I must stress that these are only suggestions and ideas for you to consider. Barbara Fix, author of *Survival: Prepare Before Disaster Strikes*, recommends setting up caches[145] as a form of

---

[145] Caches are collections of items of the same type stored in a hidden or inaccessible place (i.e., a gold cache, foreign currency cache, a weapons cache, or an emergency drinking

insurance for a worst-case scenario. Her examples pertain to food but can easily be applied to currency. Fix suggests hiding valuable assets in plain sight like boxes marked for 'Tax Records' or 'Family Pictures.'[146] If you're industrious, you can also build false bottoms in a sofa, a bed or chair. Hiding coins in coffee cans with the coffee still in them is another idea. Put currencies in sealed sandwich bags or another type of wrapping that will keep out moisture. Remember, currency is made out of paper. Keeping currency safe from fire is just as important as keeping it safe from moisture. The containers or boxes used should also be fireproof.

CRYPTO CURRENCIES

In the simplest terms, crypto currency is a digital currency that operates outside of our current banking system and the central banks.[147] Like paper currency, it operates as a medium of exchange for goods and services. Crypto currency uses technology called cryptography to secure financial transactions. Cryptography is a secure form of electronic communication that uses algorithms to encrypt and decrypt data by using secret keys.[148] Crypto currencies can be viewed on ledgers or on a list of financial records using block-chain technology.

Bitcoin should be part of your currency kit. Bitcoin was the first and remains the most popular crypto currency. Four thousand types of crypto currencies currently exist. These are sometimes referred to as altcoins (alternatives to Bitcoin). Many of these crypto currencies are platforms for new kinds of services

---

water cache, etc.).
146 For more information, see Michael T. Snyder and Barbara Fix, Get Prepared Now!: Why a Great Crisis is Coming and How You Can Survive It (New York: Bloomsbury Press, 2015).
147 Editors, "Cryptocurrency," Oxford Dictionaries, updated November 2018. https://en.oxforddictionaries.com/definition/cryptocurrency (accessed November 23, 2018).
148 Sarah Simpson, "Cryptography Defined/Brief History," Laits, Spring 1997. http://www.laits.utexas.edu/~anorman/BUS.FOR/course.mat/SSim/history.html (accessed November 25, 2018).

and technology. Know that this market is still in its infancy. I liken it to the Wild West days of nineteenth century America. That being said, God has shown me that crypto currencies will be a mechanism for bartering and wealth transfer when the banking system collapses. Citizens in multiple countries (even third world countries) already use bitcoin to transact business. I believe the crypto market volatility will smooth out over the next 5 to 10 years, as the platform continues to evolve.

From an investment perspective, trading crypto currencies for the sole purpose of making a profit is very risky. For the purposes of this book, I only suggest accumulating crypto currencies as a safe harbor for bartering purposes. People will need a way to transact business and having Bitcoin and a few altcoins will put the reader at an advantage if digital currency transactions become more popular and widespread in the world market.

Of the thousands of crypto currencies available today, I suggest acquiring Bitcoin first. I also propose using Coinbase, especially for novices. Coinbase is one of the most popular platforms used for the purchase, transfer, and sale of crypto currencies. Coinbase continually adds altcoins to their platform. To buy and hold, I suggest starting with the following crypto currencies:

- ✓ Bitcoin (BTC)
- ✓ Bitcoin Cash (BCH)
- ✓ Ethereum (ETH)
- ✓ Litcoin (LTC)

I liken these coins to the staples one would invest in through the stock market, such as oil, food (Nabisco, General Mills), and other commodities. Although all crypto currencies have some volatility, the above coins will likely maintain a longer shelf life and all have a strong trading base. The above coins were among the first to hit the market. Their platforms, although different, are strong and are used in many countries around the world.

WHAT SHOULD YOU DO NOW?

Piggy Banks – Many people have "piggy banks," coffee cans, mason jars, and other types of containers with money and coins stashed at home. When the United States enters into hyperinflation, U.S. dollars and especially coins will become worthless. The exception will be coins that contain a portion of silver. Below is a chart to show the type of coin and the years when the coins were minted with silver. With silver coins or sometimes referred to as junk coins you will want to retain for yourself or take them to a silver dealer rather than cashing them in at a bank.

Pennies minted between 1909-1958 and again between 1959-1982 hold about 95% copper. If metals are increasing in value, then these pennies may actually retain their value rather than become worthless.

The remaining coins can be converted into another asset. These funds can be the starting point for what's going into your Bridge Currency Kit™ or used to purchase food for storage, or any other emergency needs. The point is to take extra funds that you have on hand, and while they still hold value, trade them for something that will be more valuable in the future.

Silver Content (Partial List)	1942-1945	1932-1964	1946-1964	1965-1970	1971-1974
Nickels (Jefferson)	35%				
Dime			90%		
Quarter		90%			
Half Dollar			90%	40%	
Dollar			90%		40%
Bicentennial Quarters "S" Mark				40%	
Bicentennial Halfs "S" Mark				40%	

CHAPTER 14

Financial Triage

> "A budget is telling your money where to go instead of wondering where it went."
>
> Dave Ramsey[149]

I coined the term 'financial triage' several years ago to deal with some tough financial situations in my own life. When many patients arrive at a medical facility all at once, first responders have to determine the order in which patients will be treated. To triage these patients is to assign priority for treatment to each one based on the urgency of their medical needs, while taking into consideration the likelihood of each person's survival when medical resources are not sufficient to treat everyone immediately. This process of medical triage is used when emergency rooms are overrun with mass-disaster

---

[149] Dave Ramsey, "What is a Budget," Ramsey Solutions, January 2019. https://www.daveramsey.com/blog/what-is-a-budget (accessed February 15, 2019).

victims and in battlefield hospitals during times of war.[150]

Financial triage, then, is a way to determine how to use limited financial resources when there are not enough funds to cover all of your bills. Putting a financial triage system into place helped me make logical decisions about how to weather tough financial times. Specific planning also helped me push away fear. I am not saying that I always made correct decisions, but I learned from every situation. Thus, when I later faced a similar situation, I made adjustments more quickly, and became better at making the right financial decisions.

For example, there was a time when I lost my employment and my bills included: credit cards, a mortgage, a car payment, utilities, and grocery expenses. I did not have enough money to pay for it all. So, I had to decide: what do I pay? The answer will not be the same for everyone. It will depend on your individual circumstances. For example, if a person lives near decent public transportation system, he or she might decide to let go of the car payment for a short period of time, or possibly to sell the car. When financial triage becomes necessary, credit card payments are always the last bill that I pay. Maintaining a home is generally the priority. That being said, moving into something that is less expensive per month or taking in boarders may be a better option than spending your hard-earned savings to maintain the same lifestyle.

I should also mention that during financial triage, survival is the main consideration. Credit rating is not a consideration when you are trying to feed yourself and your family. If you are able to make payments within the 30-day time period to keep

---

150 Editors, "Triage," Merriam Webster Online, updated January 2019. https://www.merriam-webster.com/dictionary/triage (accessed January 28, 2019).

a late payment from appearing on your credit report, then you are not in financial triage. You are doing an urgent care move rather than a battlefield triage move. Financial triage is deciding between paying for gas, paying a cell phone or utility bill, and not having enough to pay all of them within a 30-day period.

I have learned that if I negotiate a payment arrangement with service providers ***prior*** to a service being shut off, then I can save on both late fees and reconnection fees. Bartering for payment arrangements also <u>buys time</u>. On more than one occasion, I have pushed making a payment to the very last date possible. Something has always come through financially in enough time for me to make that payment. I rely heavily on the Lord to supply my needs. He has always come through for me.

Many people, who never went through tough financial situations previously, may experience this for the first time when the economy collapses. For many, this could cause much fear and stress. Developing a plan **now** while there is time to prepare, will reduce such fear and make the resulting stress much easier to deal with.

When I taught Personal Financial Management at the University of Phoenix, the provided curriculum stated that people should put away 3 to 6 months' worth of expenses for emergency situations. In order to accomplish this goal, I first taught my students how to accurately calculate their monthly expenses, and then how to triage their bills. Financial triage means assessing which living expenses are actually necessary, as opposed to desired for lifestyle maintenance. The definition of needs in relation to wants will vary from person to person but the concept is about prioritizing during tough economic times.

A sample budget of $2,500 in monthly expenses may include the following bills:

Housing	$1,200
Utilities	300
Cable (basic)	150
Internet	90
Cell phone	100
Food	300
Gas	200
Entertainment	70
Grooming, clothes, etc.	90
Total	**$2,500**

WHAT IF THERE IS A JOB LOSS?

For a while, a person may get unemployment insurance but the amount received is always less than his or her salaried income. Is $2,500 truly the amount one needs to spend per month when unemployed? Which expenses on the above list could be considered luxuries and eliminated or reduced? Probably the cable bill, entertainment, grooming, and clothes, can all be reduced. Also, if you own a home with multiple bedrooms, then doing a room share to bring in extra income is a possibility. Moving out and renting a room from someone else is another option. Either option could save several hundred dollars per month from your housing budget. Without a job to go to every day, gas and food expenses would decrease as well. Eating out less and cooking at home more would reduce the food bill. Our adjusted monthly expenses might be as follows:

Housing	$ 800
Utilities	300
Cable (basic)	30
Internet	90
Cell phone	100
Food	200
Gas	100
Entertainment	25
Grooming, clothes, etc.	25
Total	**$1,670**

In this example, monthly expenses have been reduced to $1,670. That's a savings of $830 every month. This budgeting strategy can be employed to reduce expenses even without a job loss. Additional savings can then be used to prepare for the impending economic collapse.

WHAT ABOUT DEBT?

Many Americans are in debt. I won't spend a lot of time on this subject except to say that as you work on getting out of debt, reserve some funds for savings, specifically for The Bridge Currency Kit™. The best way for me to relate this kit's importance is to tell you what I went through leading up to the 2008 financial crisis. In 2006 and 2007, I was aggressively working to get out of debt. Most of my debt outside of mortgage payments was credit card debt. Whenever I got paid, I put a large portion towards paying down this debt. Within 6-7 months, I paid off nearly $13,000 worth of debt. However, in the process, I neglected my savings. Then the 2008 mortgage and financial crisis happened. I was affected as were many people. I did not have as much savings to help me as I otherwise could have had, if I had not been so aggressive in paying off my bills. I could have paid off my debts at a slower rate, and increased my savings at the same time. I truly regretted the decision to go all-in on paying off debt. Had I known what was about to happen, I would have made a different decision. This time around, my eyes are wide open. There is no substitute to being prepared when a financial crisis hits.

WHAT TO DO WITH EMERGENCY SAVINGS

Budgeting experts and financial advisors often exhort us to keep 3 to 9 months' or more of emergency savings on hand. However, when the United States enters into rapid inflation, followed closely by hyperinflation, these emergency funds will lose value quickly even if they are not touched. Gas and food prices will increase swiftly, eating up emergency savings at a fast pace. In Germany's case study, those who exchanged their German Marks for foreign currency as soon as the crisis started were able to stay ahead of inflation.

I am suggesting this as a strategy. Instead of holding onto emergency savings in U.S. Dollars, exchange them for one or more of the currencies listed in The Bridge Currency Kit™. The sooner you exchange U.S. Dollars for these currencies, the more they will hold their value. Trade them back to dollars as needed and stay ahead of inflation. I am suggesting that only about one month of your emergency fund should be held in U.S. Dollars. Everything else should be in a tradable asset such as silver, food, currencies from your Bridge Currency Kit™, or crypto currencies.

By way of illustration, let's say you received $500 after the collapse, but you were not ready to spend the money. At an inflation rate of 10% per day, the purchasing power of your $500 would decrease by $150 after only three days. However, if you were to trade your $500 for an equivalent amount in Brazilian Real, one of the currencies in *the Bridge* Currency Kit™, on the day you receive it, then the outcome might be different. As the dollar decreases in value, the Brazilian Real will increase in value. We don't know at this point what the trading value between the two currencies will be, but let's assume that $500 can be exchanged for 650 BRL. If you wait a few days, the Brazilian Real will increase in value as the USD loses value. After waiting for a few days more before trading back to dollars, you would then receive more than the $500 you originally traded. How much would depend on the exchange rate for that day. This is how to retain your purchasing power during periods of hyperinflation. Note that exchanging currencies costs money, but for this illustration currency vendor fees were not calculated.

BUILDING COMMUNITY

Every family should have enough provisions for themselves for about 3 months at a minimum. Some argue that the number of months should be a lot higher. However, the amount of provision needed will depend on your location and at what time of year the economic collapse hits. For winter months, more provision will be needed in the Midwest and Northern parts of America because of the inability to grow food in that season. In the South and part of the West, where climates are warmer, residents may be able to get away with less because of their ability to grow food almost year round. The ability to store food is also a factor. Those who live in urban areas and apartments may have less space for storage than others. Where you live is something to seriously consider. When the country's economic infrastructure fails, the inability to obtain basic necessities at grocery stores will result in chaos and violence as people panic. Now may be a good time to pray about and consider relocation.

Inquire of the Lord about what items you and your family should stockpile for personal consumption and to barter. I would recommend at least 1-5 items to have on hand for bartering purposes. In the prophetic word the Lord gave me, He said what would be deemed valuable today will not be of any value during these perilous times. What we don't deem valuable, or things that we take for granted as of minor importance today, will become very valuable in the future. These items may include: Toiletries, soap, razors, lotion, first-aid kits, matches, salt, and much more. A sample list is provided at the end of the book, but it is not exhaustive. Each person must determine their own needs. Items chosen should be things that can be traded for food or other necessities like medical supplies. However, it will not do any good if everyone has the same items to trade with. Pray about items that would be unique, something needed but not easily found. Think about things that are imported into the community but would stop if transportation and the movement of goods were temporarily suspended.

Many resources exist to help you plan for the coming economic collapse. The best guidance for stockpiling comes from preppers. Preppers are people who prepare in advance for catastrophic disasters. Some may consider these people paranoid. However, preppers provide the best resources for how to survive what is coming to America. There is little agreement about what types of disasters to prepare for among preppers. What and how much to save also varies widely. That being said, I have listed a few resources below for informational purposes only. Many other resources exist, including books and YouTube videos that can help guide you.

1. Survival Blog - https://survivalblog.com/newbies/
2. Backdoor Survival - https://www.backdoorsurvival.com/
3. Prepper Website - https://www.prepperwebsite.com/
4. The Organic Prepper - https://www.theorganicprepper.com/
5. My Family Survival Plan - http://www.myfamilysurvivalplan.com/
6. New to Prepping? Be VERY Careful. - http://www.prepper-resources.com/new-to-prepping-be-very-careful-please-share/
7. Survivor Jane - http://www.survivorjane.com/
8. Preparedness Advice - https://preparednessadvice.com/
9. Seasoned Citizen Prepper - http://seasonedcitizenprepper.com/
10. The Apartment Prepper - http://seasonedcitizenprepper.com/
11. Doom And Bloom - https://www.doomandbloom.net/
12. The Survival Mom - https://www.doomandbloom.net/

CHAPTER 15

Conclusion

> *"A Joseph calling is a marketplace call that a man or woman goes through in order to become a spiritual and physical provider to others. You become known, just like Joseph became known, by the adversity you have gone through. It is a marketplace call."*
>
> J. Gunnar Olson[151]

This book serves as a written testimony of what the Lord has shown me as well as a reference guide for those who have the Joseph anointing and take this warning seriously. As of late 2018, there are many indicators in the media concerning the instability of the markets, the government shutdown, increasing tensions in the Middle East

---

[151] Os Hillman, "Six Important Stages You'll Go Through if You Carry a Joseph Anointing – A Joseph Calling," Charisma Magazine, April 27, 2017. https://www.charismamag.com/spirit/spiritual-growth/32527-6-important-stages-you-ll-go-through-if-you-carry-a-joseph-anointing (accessed February 1, 2019).

with Israel, and economic tensions in Europe due to Brexit.[152] Similar events occurred in the past. Studying previous patterns confirms that something financially devastating will happen again. The coming economic collapse will affect everyone; it will be felt worldwide. And Americans will be key players in the drama with their own heart-wrenching stories due to lack of finances, and possibly lack of food. Not since the Great Depression has the U.S. seen devastating financial times affect such large numbers of her citizens as will happen in the next economic crisis.

But in the midst of the coming hardship, there will also be miracles and testimonies of God's goodness, unfailing love, and provision. Those who prepare now, and are able to adapt when the crisis hits, will be able to weather the coming storm. These preparers or Josephs will also possibly come through the other side not only unscathed, but better off from the wealth transfer I believe God intends to usher in for His people.

I would like to conclude this book with a story:

A few years ago, a terrible storm came to a town. Local officials sent out an emergency warning that the riverbanks would soon overflow and flood nearby homes. Town residents were ordered to evacuate immediately.

A faithful Christian man heard the warning and decided to stay, saying to himself, "I will trust God and if I am in danger, then God will save me."

Neighbors came by his house and said to him, "We're leaving, please come with us!" But the man said no. "I have faith that God

---

[152] BREXIT was a referendum that the citizens of the United Kingdom voted on in 2016; a majority deciding to leave the European Union. The fallout from that vote has caused major economic instability throughout Europe.

will save me."

The faithful Christian man stood on his porch watching the water rise up the steps. Then a man in a row boat called to him, "Come into my boat, the waters are rising quickly!" But the man again said, "No thanks, God will save me. I have faith."

The man retreated to the second floor of his house as the floodwaters rose higher spilling into his living room. A police motorboat came by and saw him at the window. "We will come up and get you!" they shouted. But the man refused saying, "Go save someone else! I have faith that God will save me!"

The man climbed to the rooftop as the flood waters rose and covered the first and second floor of the house.

A helicopter spotted him and dropped a rope ladder. The rescue officer shouted pleading with the man, "Grab onto the rope ladder and I will pull you up!" But the man still refused, folding his arms tightly to his body. "No thank you! I have faith that God will save me!"

A short time later, the flood waters engulfed the house and the man drowned.

Once in Heaven, the man stood before God and asked, "I don't understand. I had great faith but You let me drown. Why didn't You save me?"

And God answered, "My son, I sent you a warning. I sent your neighbors. I sent you a row boat. I sent you a police motorboat.

And I sent you a helicopter. What more were you expecting?"[153]

God instructed me to write this book. It is my prayer that it will be an alarm sounder for the reader as well as a blessing regarding its instructions on how to prepare. I see this book as part of the beginning of a greater movement within the Body of Christ. God has not finished speaking on this subject. As long as He continues to speak to me and gives the clarion call, I will continue to obey by sharing His words with those who have ears to hear.

---

153 Adapted from "The Drowning Man," Author Unknown, The Truth Book. https://truthbook.com/stories/funny-god/the-drowning-man (accessed February 20, 2019) and Tony DuFrene (ed.), "Two Boats and a Helicopter: Thoughts on Stress Management," May 4, 2009. https://www.psychologytoday.com/us/blog/fumbling-change/200905/two-boats-and-helicopter-thoughts-stress-management (accessed February 20, 2019).

APPENDIX A
Representation of Supply and/or Stockpile List for Economic Collapse

Food	Gardening	Hygiene	Medical	Currency	Barter	Other
Food Buckets	Seeds	Wipes	First Aid kit	Gold/Silver Jewelry	Hard Liquor	Radio
Canned Goods	Soil	Soap	Over the counter drugs	Gold and Silver coins for bartering	Cigarettes	Car parts
Freeze dried cans	Bug spray	Baby wipes	Antibiotics	Sterling silverware	Guns, ammo	Tent
Rice (not brown rice), dried beans	Shovel	Hand Sanitizer	Book – "Where there is no doctor" by Werner and Gordon		Flares	Sleeping bags
Dried milk	Fertilizer	Natural Antibiotics			Propane stove	Cutting tools, Ax
MREs (meals ready to eat)	Gardening pots	Laundry soap	"Where there is no Dentist" by Murray Dickson		Spices	Lighters/Matches
Canned Tuna		Dish detergent	Physician's desk reference		Toiletries	Twine, rope
Canned chicken		Toothbrushes	Army manuals		Batteries	Shower curtain liner/for cover outdoors
Spam		Toothpaste			Compass	Clorox
Salt without iodine, Pepper		Toilet paper			Salt	Passports
Instant Oatmeal					Sugar	Bicycles
Honey and sugar, maple syrup, vanilla extract						Bleach
Coffee						Fuel
Water						Personal Skills
Flour						Lantern
Vinegar, Corn Starch						Lamp oil
Dried pasta						Lamp wicks
Cooking oil						State and City maps
						Basic tool kit
						Fishing equipment
						Candles

The Bridge is a clarion call and the starting point for communications and connections between those who desire to stay linked with the author and receive updates about information and prophecies. Please stay in touch on Twitter: @Josephs20221, or join my email list at: https://www.smore.com/83xwy-the-bridge.

ABOUT THE AUTHOR

Sonja Felder has been preparing taxes for more than 30 years. She also spent several years working as a Financial Analyst for a major corporation in Atlanta, Georgia. In 2006, Sonja earned her Master's degree in Taxation. She later moved to Southern California. After earning her Enrolled Agents' license, Sonja taught Accounting and Finance at the University of Phoenix. Currently, Sonja resides in Omaha, Nebraska where she operates her own Accounting and Tax firm.

Sonja began receiving prophecies from the Lord not long after dedicating her life to Jesus in the mid 1990's. As her relationship with the Lord grew, so did her prophetic gift. Around 2006, the prophecies Sonja received from the Lord started to include messages about the Church and the United States. Per the Lord's instructions, Sonja started documenting many of her prophecies on a blog which can be found at https://simpleservant.wordpress.com/. Sonja believes Omaha, Nebraska will become a Kingdom of God financial center in the last days.

The Bridge is a clarion call and the starting point for communications and connections between those who desire to stay linked with the author and receive updates about information and prophecies. Please stay in touch on Twitter: @Josephs20221, or join my email list at: https://www.smore.com/83xwy-the-bridge.

> "Surely the Lord God does nothing,
> Unless He reveals His secret
> to His servants the prophets.
> A lion has roared!
> Who will not fear?
> The Lord God has spoken!
> Who can but prophesy?"
> Amos 3:7-8 (NKJV)

www.ingramcontent.com/pod-product-compliance
Lightning Source LLC
Chambersburg PA
CBHW022002170526
45157CB00003B/1104